T0161186

PRAISE FOR *THE EVOLVED ENTERPRISE*

"Yanik shows entrepreneurs how re-writing the rules can create a better world." — **Sir Richard Branson, founder Virgin Group**

"Business is now the largest institution on earth and with that power comes a new responsibility and a huge new opportunity. *Evolved Enterprise* fulfills that opportunity by outlining the framework for creating a meaningful impact while growing your profits and contributing to the world."
— **Lynne Twist, author, The Soul of Money, co-founder, The Pachamama Alliance**

"Excellent & Evolutionary. Clear & Concise."
— **Richard Saul Wurman**

"Yanik Silver is a new breed of Super Hero, one who hasn't lost touch with the little boy inside. He's one of the rare few who are capable of launching between creativity, acumen, execution, and, ultimately, philanthro-capitalistic enlightenment. Right brain? Left brain? No—Yanik has right, left, front, and back firing at one time! Who does that? Evolved Enterprise offers the answer to that question and many more in riveting fashion!"
— **Frank McKinney, 5x bestselling author, including *The Tap***

"If you're satisfied standing still and being stuck with the status quo, save yourself some time and simply skip reading this book. But if you're ready to embrace the adventure of creative entrepreneurship for the new century, *Evolved Enterprise* is one of the most engaging ways I've discovered to guide you towards a more meaningful future, more fun, and better finance! All at the same time!"
— **Ari Weinzweig, co-founder Zingermans**

"I had Yanik Silver on my SiriusXM Show, and afterwards the phones were ringing off the hook. People were inspired by his insights and his compassion to do good while he does well. He is one of the most enlightened and conscious entrepreneurs I have ever met. He is someone who really gets the idea that it is important to not only make a profit but also make a difference in the lives of others! This book will help you become a better business person and a better human being!"
— **Dr. Willie Jolley, host of** *The Willie Jolley Wealthy Ways Radio Show* **and bestselling author of** *A Setback Is a Setup for a Comeback & an Attitude of Excellence.*

"...This is now one of my FAVORITE books... exactly what I needed at this specific time. Everything about the book—the content, the way it was written, the tone, the examples, everything was incredibly helpful. It's the first book I've read that communicated the concept of merging business and impact in such a clear, inspiring, and actionable way."
— **Bassima Mroe, President Sara Blakely Foundation**

"The Evolved Enterprise seems almost too good to be true. You can create a meaningful impact in the world with your business, get customers to buy more, create greater team alignment, and have a higher purpose... which all drive higher profits. Yanik Silver's thought process is incredible!"
— **Brian Smith, Founder of UGG Australia, Author of** *Birth of a Brand*

"It's time to redefine our expectations of business. This book is the blueprint that will help you drive the greatest results—for your business and for the world."
— **Blake Mycoskie, TOMS founder**

"Through free enterprise, one can benefit people all over the world... by contributing to a better way of life for all. Peace, love & happiness."
— **John Paul DeJoria, co-founder, Paul Mitchell Hair Care**

"Jeff Bezos said, 'The only danger is not to evolve.' Yanik Silver agrees, and in his new book, he shares his message, mission, and movement about how to turn transactional business into transformative, even transcendent, business. He uses compelling examples and step-by-step instructions to show how you can create an evolved enterprise that serves all involved. Brilliant." — **Sam Horn, author of POP!** *Tongue Fu*

"Yanik Silver has focused his thinking and efforts for years on helping CEOs grow companies that care about people, causes, and others as much as they do revenue and profits. His book is a must read for anyone who cares about creating a company that 'matters.'"
— **Cameron Herold, CEO, coach, and author of** *Double Double*

"Yanik Silver is a truly conscious entrepreneur who understands that creating meaning for yourself—and everyone connected to your business—is absolutely vital in the 21st century."
— **Chip Conley, former CEO of Joie de Vivre hotel group and author of PEAK and** *Emotional Equations*

"When you align the true soul of your business with more impact, meaning and happiness—you'll inevitably create greater profits."
— **Ted Leonsis, Founder, Chairman, Majority Owner and CEO of Monumental Sports & Entertainment**

"This book takes theory into practice and gives you a rare glimpse into the mind of a modern-day maverick."
— **Andrew Hewitt, founder, GameChangers500**

"Yanik Silver's *Evolved Enterprise* is the perfect blend of cutting-edge case studies and his own hard-fought business wisdom."
— **Dorie Clark, author of *Stand Out* and *Reinventing You***

"The organizations that accept your challenge to evoke in this way will be rewarded with an inspired work force and loyal customers."
— **Andy Levine, founder and chairman, Sixthman**

"There's a transformative shift in business, and what worked before is no longer an option. It's time for evolved entrepreneurs, visionary creators, and change makers to rewrite the rules of business for the 21st century."
— **Tony Hsieh, NY Times bestselling author of *Delivering Happiness* and CEO of Zappos.com, Inc.**

"...forever changed the way I look at building businesses. The future of business has changed; this book explains how."
— **Dan Martell, Angel investor and founder of Clarity.FM**

"Yanik doesn't just say you can do well by doing good. Use his thinking to make a positive difference on hunger, poverty, climate change—and your own bottom line."
— **Shel Horowitz, green/social change business consultant and award-winning author of *Guerrilla Marketing to Heal the World* and nine other books**

"Jump aboard Yanik's evolutionary train and onto the express track for learning how to be more innovative and creative with your team while having fun in the process."
— **Bill Donius, author of *Thought Revolution***

"Yanik Silver is a trailblazing visioneer who is paving the way for conscious business-minded entrepreneurs. Yanik's creative genius is his remarkable ability to articulate the process to creating an 'Evolved Enterprise,' one focused on delivering exceptional value while solving meaningful issues in the world. This book is a total game changer."
— **Wendi Blum, CEO of Success Blueprint**

"You'll get techniques, tools, and motivation to deliver meaningful impact and greater profits, and Yanik has bundled it up in a sincere, smart, and thoughtful approach. I can confidentially say that if you want to make your mark as an extraordinary entrepreneur, absorb the words of this book and act on them."
— **Adam Toren, co-founder at Small Business BIG Vision**

"The rules of business have changed. In *Evolved Enterprise*, Yanik Silver lays out the new formula for entrepreneurial success—combining purpose with profit and having fun in the process. This book is a must-read if you're looking to build an enterprise that makes a meaningful, measurable, global impact."
— **Roger James Hamilton, founder of Entrepreneurs Institute and NY Times bestselling author of *The Millionaire Master Plan***

"Step-by-step guidance to conceptualize and build an Evolved Enterprise and create a win, win, win, win for employees, customers, entrepreneurs, and the world. Yanik's unbridled passion and authenticity shine throughout the book. His accessible and evocative language left me feeling like creating an Evolved Enterprise was something I wanted and could do."
— **Alison Whitmire, President of Learning In Action Technologies, Inc. & TEDx organizer**

"A great read at a time when business as a force for good is more important than ever before in the world."
— **Jean Oelwang, President and Trustee for Virgin Unite and Senior Partner at the B Team**

Let's co-create these ideas, share more examples
and make the concepts stronger for everyone.
We're organizing a private discussion group here:

www.EvolvedEnterprise.com/resources

EVOLVED
ENTERPRISE

An Illustrated Guide to Re-Think, Re-imagine &
Re-Invent Your Business to Deliver Meaningful
Impact & Even Greater Profits

YANIK SILVER

IDEAPRESS
PUBLISHING

Ideapress Publishing

We Publish Brilliant Business Books

www.ideapresspublishing.com

All trademarks are the property of their respective companies.
Interior Layout design by Anton Khodakovsky

ISBN: 978-1-61961-348-5

PRINTED AND BOUND IN THE UNITED STATES

This book is available for bulk purchases at
www.EvolvedEnterprise.com/bulk

Acknowledgments

For my wife, Missy...thank you for being the voice of reason during the times when I needed it and also giving me enough rope to figure things out and pursue the Evolved Ecoverse.

For my children, Zack and Zoe...I've only left guideposts. My deepest wish for you is to simply follow your heart to see where it takes you and to never live your life to please anyone else.

CONTENTS

PRELUDE

"Don't regurgitate rainbows."

—YANIK SILVER

 *Are you ready to surrender your former smallness to your destiny of greatness? To fully step forward into the total transformation of your business, your life, and your legacy, knowing you won't be the same again?*

It's a scary thought because our identities are so closely aligned to WHO we think we are with our existing business or previous accomplishments.

But all of that is just "R&D" for what lies ahead.

It's not about "starting over"—it's about taking everything you've developed, built, researched, succeeded with, "failed" at, intuited, struggled through, and overcome.

Every relationship you've nurtured every network connection, goodwill cultivated, reputation built, skills developed—it's all brought you right here and right now to this moment.

And like a phoenix rising, your emergence into joyful abundance as an Evolved Enterprise is inevitable.

I was in trouble...

I needed to make payroll and pay several vendors, but we were short $70,000.00.

Not good!

Normally I'm a pretty laidback guy, but I was really pissed. Mostly I was just angry at myself for letting this happen. I don't usually have a temper, but I heaved a cereal bowl at my wall.

Damn it!

I mean, how the hell could I not fix this? I pretty much had the Midas touch with all my business ventures before. But now, something I cared so deeply and passionately about was going south...and dragging my other businesses down along with it.

By way of background, I've had eight different products and services that hit the cumulative seven-figure mark in the online space—so I knew a thing or two about what works—but the playbook had changed for me.

How did I get here?

Let's rewind a little...

Our family is one of those semi-typical immigrant success stories you hear about. My parents arrived in the U.S. from Russia in 1976 with $256 in their pockets for my parents, my grandmother, and little Yanik. They both didn't speak much English, but they were willing to work. That immigrant mentality of starting from nothing and building something was the driving force for what I've learned. I also think that is what all entrepreneurship is about—starting from nothing and creating something.

My dad was trained as a biomedical engineer back in Russia, and he went to work for a local hospital in America. Pretty quickly they told him that they were either going to fire him or he had to leave because he was moonlighting on the side repairing medical equipment for some of the private doctors' offices. So he took a risk and decided to go off on his own in 1978.

Now, growing up in a family business, you basically do all sorts of things. When I was 14 years old, he had me go out and telemarket for latex gloves that we were selling. This was the first part of the big AIDS scare, and I called on dentists. I built up my own lead base, followed up on them, and then was paid commissions when somebody bought gloves.

Then when I was 16 years old, my dad made me a deal that I could get a car (Carol the Corolla) if I went out and actually sold medical equipment and cold called on docs. While many of my friends were living at the beach, I was "stuck" selling medical equipment. (Though, looking back, I realize how much of a massive head start I got in sales and marketing education.)

It was one of my doctor clients who really gave me a giant leap forward a few years later with just one single audiotape from Jay Abraham. Jay was a big direct marketing guy who turned the lights on for me. I just kept listening to that tape over and over and over again. My friends would ride around in my car and ask, "What the hell is this stuff?" My response was "Don't worry about it." I followed Brian Tracey's advice of creating a "university on wheels" inside your car by constantly listening to learning and growth materials.

That's also the time that I got much deeper into direct response marketing. I was so fascinated by this idea that we could get people to buy without necessarily talking to them and not cold calling on them. I started learning from Ted Nicholas, Joe Sugarman, Dan Kennedy, and Gary Halbert, among others. Then all the classics from advertisers like Claude Hopkins, Maxwell Sackheim, David Ogilvy, John Caples, and more. One of my audio mentors was Earl Nightingale, and I really took his philosophy to heart that by simply studying for one hour per day on any subject, you could become an expert in three years or a world-class expert in five years. I decided to accelerate it and see what would happen if I immersed myself for hours each day.

I just kept getting deeper and deeper into this stuff and then applying it to my dad's business, where I'd write a full-page ad selling an EKG machine or fetal doppler. My dad would look at the ad and say, "Who's going to read all this?"

But people did. It literally took his business from the small regional player to more of a national player because the ads would appear across the country. We were having doctors call with their credit card numbers or even just faxing back that they wanted to buy our equipment. Before, we could only sell face to face or get appointments with them. But with the direct response advertising, we were only talking to people that were 7s, 8s, 9s, or 10s on the scale of being ready to buy.

The First Itch of Something Greater

That really opened my eyes to what's possible. Originally, I thought I was going to take over my dad's business and grow it. And just like my dad, I started moonlighting on the side, helping my doctor clients who wanted more elective cash patients outside the realm of managed care and HMOs.

The most interesting one was a dermatologist because we were dealing with cosmetic patients. I was helping him do lead generating advertising instead of just doing the same stuff that other doctors were doing: to ask for a free consult. We were giving prospective patients educational reports, creating referral systems, reactivating "lost" patients, and maximizing marketing dollars, and all of it really boosted his practice's bottom line.

Fortunately, I realized pretty quickly that there wasn't much leverage as a consultant selling my time for money. Following the advice of Dan Kennedy, I packaged up what I knew into a three-ring binder course that I sold for $900, called "How to Cash In on More Cosmetic Cases." Starting in May of 1998, I placed one tiny ad in *Dermatologic Surgery* and got 10 doctors to respond.

I sent out the first sales letters, and I heard nothing...2nd notice...still crickets. I was really unsure what to do but decided to follow the plan and send out the 3rd and final notice to these doctors. And literally on the last day of the deadline, I got one to say "yes." During those three weeks, I was running to my dad's fax machine every time it rang, and finally I saw an order come through for $900!

I was ecstatic!

But after peeling myself off the ceiling, I realized, "Oh, shit! Now I have to make it." That's when I sent back a note to the doctor saying the program was going to be republished in 30 days and we were not going to charge his card. I clocked out every single day exactly at 5:00 p.m. and went to work on my own material, many nights not leaving until 2:00 a.m. or 3:00 a.m., to finish this course.

That work paid off and led to my first publishing company, where I was working with doctors and helping them grow their practice. I was still working for my dad and remember answering my cell phone under my desk to take orders or talk to potential clients.

Looking back at this period, I was getting increasingly more frustrated because my stepbrother provided a lot of unwanted input for the ads and marketing pieces I was creating for my dad's business. My stepbrother worked there in the capacity of sales manager. Now, with some greater awareness, I can see it was a good thing because it helped spur my decision to make the move out of there.

It was a really hard call to make because it was a family company, but I knew that it was right for me, and I couldn't live my life wondering what would happen if I didn't set off on my own.

Perfect Timing

In July of 1999 I left my dad's company, and that opened up a space for something really big brewing.

The timing was really interesting because businesses were just starting to realize the Internet might be a significant profit opportunity. Frankly, I didn't even have an email address in '99, but I knew it was the next big thing. Previously, I hadn't really paid much attention to the Internet as a business possibility because it seemed like only sleazy porn sites or "get rich quick online" stuff was selling. Now it felt like there was a shift going on.

When I looked at the potential, I could see that it used a lot of the same key principles that I had already learned and developed over the years. It was all about leverage and using direct response. The Internet became just another medium for learning and applying what I'd learned—but on a much bigger leverage scale.

I firmly believe your questions create your possibilities. Looking at the Internet as a potential opportunity, I asked myself, *"How do I create a fully automatic Web site that provides an incredible value and makes me money while I sleep?"*

I wanted to create something that worked on autopilot, made money regardless of where I was in the world, and provided an incredible value to the customer.

I literally woke up at three o'clock in the morning, and it just came to me. I nudged my wife, Missy, and said, "Mis, Mis, get up! I've got the idea!" Like any entrepreneur, I always had tons of ideas.

She grumbled, "Just go back to sleep."

I couldn't do it and muttered something like, "No, no. This is going to be great!"

Instead of rolling over, I actually jumped out of bed, registered the domain InstantSalesLetters.com, and got to work on it. I had no technical skills to put up a site (still don't), but I didn't let that stop me. I simply started working on creating fill-in-the-blank formulas from the best sales letters I'd developed for my dad's business, the doctor clients, and a few other clients in different industries I'd picked up.

I still remember waking up and seeing $29.95 sitting in my inbox. It was pretty awesome, and the funny thing is, we didn't even have our online merchant account ready, but someone had found our site and ordered.

Within the first month, I made about $1,800. In the third month, it was around $7,800, then $9,400, and on track to do six figures within six months. That's when people started asking me, "How did you do this, and is there any way you can teach me how to do what you've done?"

I didn't expect it, but it turned into my next transition—helping others take their content or expertise or knowledge and selling it on the Internet to make money from it that way.

I loved working with so many incredible people and helping them take their passions, knowledge, interests, expertise, and message out into the world by selling content and information. These students built five-, six-, seven- and even eight-figure-plus businesses in pretty much every conceivable field with my help.

Over the years I've had so many people walk up and tell me how I've changed the trajectory of their life, and that was incredibly rewarding, but there was still something missing.

The Success Trap

From the outside, most people would think I had achieved total success. I was making a LOT of money online by truly helping people. I had built up a great reputation in the marketplace, drove a cool car, had an incredible family, lived in a nice neighborhood, etc.

Don't get me wrong, I was (and still am) extremely grateful and appreciative for everything I had, but **I just wasn't totally happy.**

Maybe you've experienced the same thing…

You've "made it" but realize there's something more.

Perhaps you have a nagging notion you can't shake that you were designed for greater things. You want to fully put ALL your talents, passion, and resources into something bigger. Maybe you discount all of this as burnout, but it's much bigger than that.

It usually starts with a sense of discontent or frustration. Or a sense of being bored with what's going on in your business.

Of course, you could continue to plug away, but you know in your heart that will just slowly eat away at your soul. **You ~~want~~ need to make a leap into the next chapter but aren't sure you can without sacrificing everything you've built.**

And that lack of enthusiasm carries over to your team, your work, and your customers. Truly everything. You're either going to subconsciously sabotage your business or your life to make it change unless you're aware of what's going on. That's when you go looking for creative (and sometimes self-destructive) outlets to compensate for not being totally engaged. Following your true heart's calling is never wrong— but frequently scary!

I know because I've been there.

That's why, a little over eight years ago, I made my next biggest transition from "just" being an Internet marketer teaching and selling my own products. My criteria was pretty simple. I asked myself the big question: **"Would I be happy and totally fulfilled 10 years from now doing what I was doing now?"**

The answer was a resounding and booming "NO!"

I knew my greatest contribution lay somewhere else with everything so far being the setup for something greater. I had stopped growing and stopped being passionate about what I was doing.

These frustrations led me to do a lot of journaling and reflection.

Steve Jobs talked about keeping all the passions in your life because you cannot connect the dots looking forward but only looking back.

My discovery was that I was happiest when I was actively engaged in three areas. As shortcuts, I called them make more, have more fun, and give more. And interestingly enough, I found that each of these areas affected the others. For example, the more fun I had, the more my income might go up; or the more I gave, the more income I'd create, etc. This concept looked like this:

After creating this foundation, it's really been a part of everything moving forward.

Originally, my idea that came from journaling stemmed from my own desire to hang out with other successful entrepreneurs and do wild adventures together. I'd combine it with business building and something charitable mixed in. I wanted to combine everything I really liked together and called the company Maverick Business Adventures®, with the appropriate acronym of MBA.

I had bootstrapped my first venture with a couple hundred bucks out of a one-bedroom apartment, but for this one, I was going to do it "right."

I would hire a real team, we would go first-class on the branding, and I'd really invest in the business in all the ways I never did before.

I'm a big believer in forced deadlines to create action, so I set our first Maverick Business Adventures® trip to go Baja racing in Mexico in January 2008.

Baja racing is one of my favorite adventures and holds deep personal meaning for me. My friend, Corey Rudl, first introduced me to this experience only a few months before a tragic racing accident claimed his life.

This kind of wild adventure developed powerful connections in a totally different setting. We ended up becoming friends with several high-level CEOs (including one NASDAQ-listed company) who were also on the trip. Corey and I talked about business and life and a lot about wild adventures we wanted to do, like flying MiGs together. Unknowingly, that trip was a big spark to create Maverick Business Adventures®.

Even though the destination and the epic activity were locked down, I still wasn't quite sure how I was going to pull it off. Would enough people come? Could I line up a celebrity guest or not? But I took the leap figuring it'd work out, and it did. For this inaugural trip, we had motorcycle mogul Jesse James as our special guest.

Attendees loved it, and I'm proud to say several of the entrepreneurs who went on that very first Baja trip are still active in Maverick even as it's changed and evolved quite a bit.

Here's the description I wrote about Maverick originally—as you can see, a much greater focus on the adventure and experience:

Maverick Business Adventures® combines truly unique, one-of-a-kind experiences with exclusive business building, high-level networking & powerful connections. It's the first and only membership of successful entrepreneurs & top achievers to come together and really LIVE life to the fullest.

It's all about...

- *Unique, one-of-a-kind experiences.*
- *Big adventures.*
- *Powerful connections that happen outside of the "normal" business setting.*
- *Business building & high-level networking.*
- *Plus lots of fun (that's even tax deductible).*

I loved the idea of Maverick Business Adventures!

And that was part of the problem.

You have to be careful to keep some of that passion in check with **Maverick rule #16: "Bootstrap: Having too much capital leads to incredible waste and doing things using conventional means."** Yes, even that was one of the rules from my 34 *Rules for Maverick Entrepreneurs* book, and I didn't follow it! (A very loud "do as I say not as I do" seems to ring in my ears here.)

We lost about $30k on this first trip, and then in short order, I sunk about $400,000.00 in before Missy finally asked what I was doing.

I was so excited about this project that I made some expensive hiring mistakes, bringing in six-figure people before we needed them or ones who couldn't perform within the resources of a startup.

What's more, I didn't stop soon enough to evaluate the business model. It was all about the trip, and the margins on an excursion are so much thinner than selling information as I had before. There was a small membership fee but not really enough to cover everything we were doing and the team I had hired.

I rationalized by telling myself it was an investment because this was a different type of business and that it might take some time to break even.

I've learned the universe will continue to bonk you on the head with increased severity if you don't figure it out. I had done a lot of financial juggling, like having one company pay for a sponsorship for another instead of letting it stand on its own two feet. But the day I chucked my cereal bowl at the wall across the room, I knew I had to face reality.

It took selling my Aston to pay for payroll to get my attention. (I still have a small dent on the wall as a reminder to me.) It was pretty much either sell my car or my ticket to space on Virgin Galactic for extra cash to help the company through the crunch. I figured cars come and go—but a ticket to space is pretty awesome.

After finally realizing the downward financial trajectory of the company, it forced me to change up the business model significantly. We adjusted the cost structure while also updating benefits and services to members to include several structured retreats per year.

Another big change was the name to **Maverick1000** to more accurately reflect the evolution of bringing together 1,000 game-changing entrepreneurs. It was about a global collective of individuals who not only wanted to grow themselves and their business but also wanted to have a genuine impact in the world while having fun in the process...**truly changing the way business is played.**

It was a longer process than I thought, but we did turn the company around, and now I'm proud to say it's solidly in the black.

Looking back at this experience, I'm actually incredibly grateful for not getting it "right" the first go around.

Is Your WHY Big Enough?

I'm thankful for those experiences because it forced me to truly decide if the vision for what we were building was worth it or not. If I was just creating a fun adventure company, then, no, it wasn't worth it. It was my love for a bigger mission that kept me going to figure out how to make it work.

I realized what I originally wanted to build wasn't nearly as impactful or compelling as the revised vision for the Maverick "Eco-verse" with the three interconnected hubs:

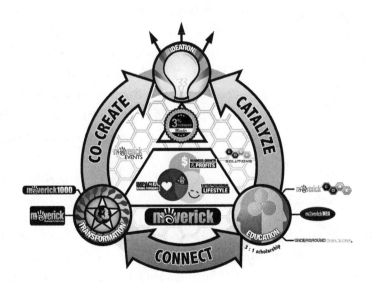

Plus, it's pretty clear that if I didn't have those bumps and stumbles instead of the fast growth curve like most of my other ventures, I wouldn't be "going back to the drawing board" to create something even better.

From an elevated point of view looking backwards, this was the absolute best thing for me. (Though I probably wouldn't agree with this at the time.)

On one hand, I was totally disengaged from my publishing company, so it's not surprising it continued going down. On the other side, my heart was with my Maverick venture, but it wasn't profitable yet. I kept feeling there was something better but was extremely frustrated by not being able to put it together.

Honestly, it was sometimes hard to look around at colleagues and friends who were having huge launches and paydays, but I wasn't willing to keep playing the same game. As entrepreneurs, our self-worth is often tied up with our bank accounts or business success. And this keeps compounding when things aren't going well in your company. Trust me, it would have been easy to go back to doing what I've always done and let those "golden handcuffs" get tighter and tighter. But I knew there was something more.

It took me going deep within to seek the answers and forge the true path forward by developing the principles of the Evolved Enterprise™. Frankly, I almost went out of business before I decoded this business model, and I don't want you to go through the same if I can help it.

14

The Cosmic Alarm Clock

There seems to be a divine timing to every level of awakening, and everybody goes through it on their own schedule and in their own way. You can't hurry it.

A few years back my daughter, Zoe, gave me the best example of how to think about this. She really, really wanted a "wiggly" tooth so bad. She kept checking her teeth, but nothing was going on. Finally, she lost her first tooth a few months after her sixth birthday, and four more followed in quick order. I commissioned Zoe to draw this poignant moment for you:

This is a perfect illustration that everything comes at the right time.

Fact is, we can either resist this "cosmic alarm clock" or lean into and embrace the transition into something bigger and better.

You probably hear it already or else you wouldn't be reading this.

Nearly every successful entrepreneur I know has gone through or has grappled with burnout or even depression. I think by nature entrepreneurs are inspired, passionate, and many times a bit (or a lot) ADHD, and all of this contributes to a feeling of malaise or frustration. I've gone through it and have come out on the other side several times.

Lately I'm seeing a lot of Maverick members and colleagues in a state of transition. Maybe it's because I've personally done this and come out on the other side that I'm seeing it more and more—but I'm not so sure. It truly feels like accomplished entrepreneurs want to know "What's next?"

The same thing that got you where you are now won't necessarily get you to the next destination on your journey. The only way to grow is to continually express your deepest essence of your greatest gifts.

Let me ask you a potentially big question...

Do you want to just push more water down the river

or

do you actually want to change the flow of the river?

I know this might be a little strange, but have you ever felt like you're destined for greatness? No, not in an egotistical type of way—but simply in a quiet, knowing way that you've been tapped to contribute something more. I've always heard that quiet voice in my ear but also the devastating echo of feeling like I could fall short of my potential.

I believe your life changes in three ways:

1. From the people you meet
2. From the books and resources you study
3. From the experiences you have

And through the unique collisions of big ideas and incredible individuals, we can co-create something meaningful, a true, interconnected *Destiny of Greatness*. Quite frankly, the bigger the future you are working on creating, the more support, resources, trusted input, connections, and energy renewal you'll need beyond the "ordinary."

We grow either through joy or pain.

Pain and frustration in your business are the guardrails to keep you moving toward joy. **And joy is the open door to your next greatest chapter of work that matters.** You can have narrow guardrails or really loose ones and experience more pain. Either way, joy will be the compelling emotion that pulls us forward.

Today, I'm more content and happier than ever, including understanding myself on a deeper level. I'm so excited for you to join me on this journey to uncover your biggest contribution and the true soul of your greatest work. Together we'll walk the path and put these counterintuitive concepts into practice.

The Evolved Enterprise is about identifying the true "soul" of your venture that delivers an exponential impact and profound profit.

Not only can this concept grow your bottom line but it can actually create a sustainable competitive advantage; re-ignite everything you do with more joy, happiness, and meaning to fulfill a higher mission.

Yes, in many ways, I'm an accomplished entrepreneur with 15+ years growing my ventures, but in so many ways, I'm just starting. As a work in progress, I feel like the advance scout who stands on the shoulders of other mentors, leaders, and advisors. And we'll walk to the edge and jump together...

CHAPTER ONE

FROM TRANSACTIONAL TO TRANSFORMATIONAL TO TRANSCENDING BUSINESS

Imagine a whole new way for your venture to actually align with your head, your heart, and your higher purpose (plus your happy inner child).

This is a counterintuitive blueprint to create a *"baked-in"* impact across your entire company by delivering an exceptional customer experience, creating a culture of fully engaged team alignment, and actually driving your bottom line!

There's no doubt—we've come to a transformative moment...

What's worked before is no longer an option. It's time for Maverick entrepreneurs, visionary creators, change makers, and impactful leaders to rewrite the rules of business for the 21st century.

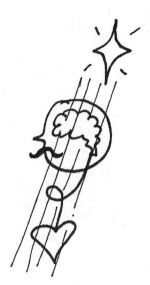

What if?

- ✓ You could catalyze a community of raving fans who eagerly wanted to spread and share your brand?

- ✓ You could attract "A-players" and empower your team around a greater mission?

- ✓ You could deliver a true impact (not just "giving back") that built a legitimate competitive advantage?

- ✓ You could scale with key distribution partners, celebrity endorsements and more press coverage?

- ✓ Business was leveraged as a multiplier for good—co-creating something great?

This is a journey to re-discover the true "soul" of business expanded—and why profits, greater happiness, and more meaningful impact are surprisingly interconnected within an Evolved Enterprise.

I believe there is a seismic shift going on, and I predict that businesses without a core IMPACT will be at a competitive disadvantage in four to seven years (or less).

The Future of Business Has Changed, and This Will Forever Change the Way You Do Business

The Evolved Enterprise is about creating (or re-creating) a company that authentically comes straight from your true essence, is wrapped around a meaningful impact, and then develops the community, culture, and creation in total alignment.

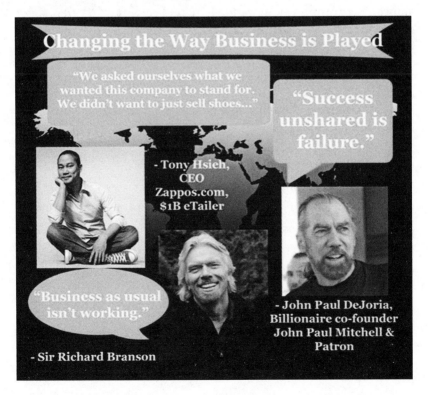

It's not just me. Many of the Maverick icons I've been fortunate to learn from and connect with truly believe business can mean something more:

And the most interesting part is that all of this is actually good for business in ALL ways. In the exceptional book *Firms of Endearment*, the authors show how firms that follow these principles have outperformed the S&P 500 by 1000% over 10 years.

That's pretty solid, right?

This is happening from the outside in with customer buying criteria changing and from the inside out with employees. Data from a recent Kone study showed consumers are more likely to switch brands to a product associated with a good cause, given similar quality and pricing.

New research from Nielsen shows 58% of global consumers (in 58 different countries) are willing to pay more for goods and services from companies that make a difference.

And then, from the inside out, employment surveys show that millennials are willing to get paid less to work for a company that has a core mission or purpose to what they do. In other research, I've seen companies that integrate a genuine impact into what they do experiencing an average 11% increase in sales versus their competitors.

"Businesses Who Ignore This Trend Will Be On Life Support In 4-7 Years..."

Forbes

This is your blueprint to re-think, re-create, and re-work business as usual.

Perhaps you're thinking, *This is just "giving back," right?*

Bzzzz...wrong!

Frankly, I admit I was incorrect about this too...

I used to say "give back" was one of the key concepts of the Maverick Entrepreneur philosophy. (It even says so right on the cover of my *34 Rules for Maverick Entrepreneurs* book: "Make More Money, Have More Fun and Give More Back.")

I've now realized this isn't quite right.

With my background as a copywriter, I'm pretty careful about most of the words I choose. In fact, it's your words (and even your internal dialogue) that have a tremendous impact on how you think, feel, and behave. By saying, "giving back," this implies entrepreneurs, like us, have taken something.

Let's think about that for a second...

> **I assert that entrepreneurs and businesses can only succeed by providing and delivering value.**

Period.

End of story.

It's simply a universal law. In fact, one of my core values in my very first journal said, *"I get rich by enriching others 10x – 100x what they pay me in return."* There's no other way that it could possibly occur, because in the long run, the marketplace is always self-correcting.

The notion of "giving back" seems to echo an undeserving indebtedness or even guilt for success. Should you begrudge entrepreneurs like Steve Jobs, Richard Branson, or Bill Gates for their wealth?

Absolutely not.

Each one of them created immense value that's exponentially in proportion to what they've received. (And that's not even counting the thousands of jobs, additional utility, new startups piggybacking on their success, etc.)

My friend and real estate artist/philanthropist, Frank McKinney, sums it up with a quote he's told our group in Haiti: *"We have to be careful not to weaken the strong in order to strengthen the weak."*

At our core, entrepreneurs are simply growth-oriented innovators and value creators. They almost can't help themselves. Take Bill Gates for instance. Aside from his impact on micro-computing, I believe his greatest contribution going forward will be around the Gates Foundation, eradicating disease, and driving new educational initiatives.

And he's not alone. Other billionaires are not content to just "give back." **They're giving forward by applying entrepreneurial talent, energy, and capital to solve some of the biggest issues facing the globe.** But you don't have to be at the level of a Gates or Branson to make a difference. Today, a group of 21st century entrepreneurs are leading the way to change the way business is played and even the rules by which we keep score. Who says it's only about one measurement on your P&L?

Frank calls this rule #33 in his awesome book, *Make It Big*.

Rule #33: You cannot brighten another's path without lighting your own.

"When you make altruism part of your business, your path will be brightened not by the publicity, nor the recognition of your good corporate citizenship, nor by the increased strength and cooperation of your team at work, it will be brightened inside your own head and heart. It will keep your success connected to something much bigger. It will allow you to feel good about making it big because you're making it big for others too."

This is a pretty perfect sentiment here. By having success in your business, you can create more and more success (automatically baked in) for everybody.

Business can become one of the biggest levers for good—while actually being good for business.

This is so much more than making a donation or "giving back." There is a deep inner connectedness between what brings you joy and happiness, how you create impact, and where profits come from.

Caveat: You cannot simply believe if you are "doing good" with your business that there's no need for a profitable and pragmatic business model. That's a recipe for quickly spiraling into anxiety and stress without the security of a strong financial foundation.

A lot of well-intended social entrepreneurs suffer from this thinking, but an evolved entrepreneur doesn't need to.

Yes, you have to put your full heart into products and services—but ALSO your full effort into ethically persuading the right prospects to buy.

It's not enough to believe the world should beat a path to your door because you are doing something wonderful via your impact. You still require smart marketing and promotion. However, the real ace up your sleeve is the multiplier effect of an Evolved Enterprise.

This is the perfect storm.

And that's why I want to hand you the greatest competitive advantage available to small businesses with the new business model I discovered—the hard way—that changed everything.

Evolved Enterprise™ Framework

Let's take a look at each section of the Evolved Enterprise, and then we'll explore it in more detail as we go.

The core is really about your personal evolution (**YOU**). The better you get at knowing yourself and what truly makes you happy and feel fully utilized and contributing in a meaningful way, the more you'll be delivering your greatest work. Business can really reflect your true essence and your true calling of who you actually are.

And what makes this most interesting is it's not a linear progression of working on yourself first and then working on the other pieces. It's not a 1-2-3 process. It's all continuously going on in a holographic way, where one change here actually affects the whole.

Moving outward with the Evolved Enterprise is the **Cause** wrapped around your authentic big WHY. Why are you doing what you're doing, and where is your impact focused? Your mission makes your business both alluring and attention getting.

Our why is *"Changing the way business is played."* (The word "played" is included to highlight a bit of fun here too.)

And this fits into the bigger picture of my personal lifetime mission:

> *I connect and catalyze Maverick entrepreneurs & visionary leaders to co-create innovative business models and new ideas to solve 100 of the world's most meaningful issues by the year 2100.*

That's a pretty tall order—but one that I'm willing to put forth my resources, energy, and talents toward. Truly something I think everything I do can line up against.

Culture is next. This is where you want to think about your team's evolution. Defining core values and actually living them is a big part of the culture. This is either going to be intentional or via osmosis, but there is always a culture to any organization. Honestly, I previously thought culture was B.S. and only for big companies, but I've since realized it makes a huge difference if you want to accomplish something grand.

Let's move on to **Community**. That's your customers/clients/members, and we'll spend a whole lot of time on this covering "Community Code 2.0." It's about creating a new identity and giving your customers a chance to be part of something bigger so they can spread your marketing message.

And finally, we have **Creation**, representing your product or service. How do you "bake in" your impact? How do we make something meaningfully different? How could it be marketed authentically and for real? And what is the significant story you would like shared? These are all questions we'll tackle in the upcoming sections.

So What's Next?

If this resonates with you, it's time to step into your true destiny of greatness...

You're being tapped for your talents, capabilities, and gifts to help open up a new era of evolved entrepreneurship. You're needed as an emissary to lift and transform the notion of what business can truly do and be.

I would even go so far as to say it's not an accident you're reading this material at this particular moment...

Together, we can collectively create the tipping point for entrepreneurs, communities, and organizations to align their heads and hearts for utilizing the massive economic leverage of business.

Then your successful example becomes the catalyst for others in your industry and marketplace. Plus, it's amplified and leveraged by the ever-widening circles, networks, and ripples of other Evolved Enterprises.

Entrepreneurial Artistry

Entrepreneurship can be the ultimate expression of artistry and love if you let it...

I believe your company can be your canvas when you bring forward your greatest work that really matters. It takes a high degree of talent to combine these Evolved Enterprise elements in unique ways, elegant business models, and team alignment, and then bring in your full heart.

What if greater happiness, more meaningful impact, and increased profits are ALL surprisingly interconnected?

Inside these pages, you'll see a lot of exciting examples of companies that are getting this at all different levels and are making the Evolved Enterprise framework work for them in a big way.

Just be open to what I'm going to share with you because on the surface, this appears to be *way* too good to be true. You've probably already seen some of these innovative companies and wondered how they grew so fast. These upstarts have come out of nowhere and cracked the code for making a real difference, recruiting & keeping "A-players," developing ultra-loyal customers, scaling quickly, and growing profits— all seemingly effortlessly. It's no wonder they've also become media and PR darlings, which only fuels their growth even more.

Sounds pretty darn terrific, right?

It is.

And you can have it happen too because the positive changes are practically inevitable when you start applying the Evolved Enterprise framework to your business idea or current venture. There's a revolution happening, and we're just at the beginning of something monumental. So strap in, and let's go...

CHAPTER TWO

THE 3 EVOLVED ENTERPRISE™ IMPACT LEVELS

Level I: Transactional

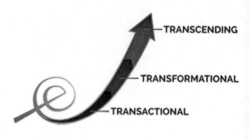

Transactional is pretty much exactly as you would think, a transaction. Its official definition is *"a one-time instance of buying or selling something; a business deal."* Not very compelling, right? And that's the way most enterprises still operate—at the transactional level. There's commoditization, little customer loyalty, and most of your team merely going through the paces.

Previous studies have shown that 70% of workers are either not engaged or actively disengaged...meaning they are actively trying to sabotage your business. And actually, new numbers I've seen from Gallup show this percentage is increasing to 87%. But this completely changes if you believe it's your duty to help everyone show up as their greatest selves and bring their full heart and soul to your venture.

At a Transactional level, many companies still may want to make an impact, but it might look like providing a percentage to a charity or a portion from every purchase going to a cause. That's fine, and it actually raises sales in many cases, as I've seen repeatedly using split testing. However, unless there's an authentic tie-in, all of this could just come across as a marketing tactic.

Many larger corporations think about Corporate Social Responsibility and allocate a budget for their "good works" and community service. Again, this is better than nothing—but I really dislike the notion of a "responsibility" or "giving back," as I referenced earlier.

A business might even have a volunteer day where their team members go build a house or contribute in the community. Yes, this is a wonderful notion, but it could be something so much bigger and integrated authentically into the culture.

Level II: Transformational

Here, the identity of your customers, team, and even the business itself develops, changes, and flourishes. At this level, you are curating a community of raving fans and advocates to spread your message. The good news here is that you'll actually require less traditional paid advertising and marketing. Plus, your team feels like they are part of something bigger and can see the authentic impact you've built in.

At the Transformational level, there is a significantly more unified and embedded notion of how and where the impact is created. **It infuses everything.** Yes, perhaps you still might do a percentage or dollar amount for every purchase, but there's more meaning and connection to the reason behind it.

Let's go back to our volunteer day example. It's not just about planting trees or building a house at this level; it's about expanding and sharing your organization's unique value. There would be a more comprehensive involvement with any organization you help, perhaps through mentoring, talent exchange, expertise provided, resource allocation, etc. You start considering what is the highest and best use of your team.

Now everybody involved is truly part of something bigger. And at our deepest core, that's what we all want.

At the Transformational level, the vision is honed and honored to enroll partners, suppliers, investors, team members, and customers into the big picture. Every product or service sold becomes something greater than just another transaction. You start figuring out how to "bake in" an impact with every purchase using one of the eleven impact models we'll cover.

Here, the thinking in an organization even transforms.

You may start considering every part of your business that has leverage to create an impact. It might be how your supply chain operates and where opportunities exist for a cause partner to provide labor or products. As one small example, we worked with Opportunity Village, an entrepreneurial non-profit in Las Vegas that provides job training and programs for disabled individuals. For our final Underground® seminar, we had them stuff all the attendee bags. It was an easy change and an existing cost we just re-allocated. Simple.

At this level, your scoreboard also evolves into keeping track of your impact delivered instead of just one profit measurement. (And the wonderful thing is this actually drives the bottom line, so it's a really exciting cross-connection.)

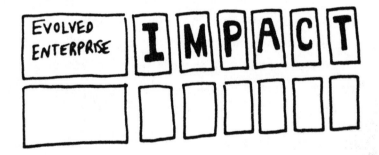

"The Scoreboard That Matters"

If entrepreneurs really explored their reason why, it's never really about the money—it's the freedom, peace, and security. And at a higher level, it's knowing you're making an impact, utilizing your talents, being creative, etc.

We can creatively create impact goals that have byproducts that force more profitability and success.

So what do you measure?

One of the most widely known examples of Evolved Enterprises would be TOMS Shoes with their "buy one – give one" model. Using this model, they can track the number of shoes given away so they've got an easy measurement of their impact. For instance, if the goal was to give away one million pairs of shoes, then as a byproduct, they'd have to sell one million pairs of shoes at a profit.

The last time I talked to Blake Myscoskie, the founder of TOMS, he told me they had given away 35,000,000 pairs of shoes. (That also means they've profitably sold 35,000,000 pairs!) And now their buy one–give one model has grown to include other products beyond shoes.

Pretty powerful!

Hang tight because in the next chapter we'll look at 11 different impact models and what we can measure as an integrated part of the Evolved Enterprise.

Level III: Transcending

This is the highest level of moving beyond what a business is even considered to a deeper essence of matching the company's true nature. I would even call it the "soul" of your venture. The thinking here is considering leverage, multipliers, platform, and interconnected eco-systems. It's more about partnering, co-creation, and the synergistic qualities that benefit each and every collaborator.

My friend, Tony Hsieh, CEO of Zappos, gets this in a big way! He has built a culture that is truly world class. They got to the transformational stage around what it meant for their team to bring their full selves to work. The core values of Zappos centered on delivering happiness, and it showed up everywhere.

Now, it might have been enough to just stick to that since they created a transformative impact on all the team members, suppliers, and many of the customers that bought from them. But there's a bigger game. Tony came up with the idea of spreading their innovations and culture philosophy to other business owners and leaders through their Zappos Insights division. That's where you would go on a field trip to the office, see the culture at work, and work through what it means to your business. It's a significant multiplier to have an influence and effect on other business owners that bring a little bit of that Zappos culture to their teams and offices.

However, this is just one of the ways they're transcending their category.

Another multiplier was Tony's book, *Delivering Happiness*, as a way to spread their transformative message to others beyond their own team and customers. Oh, and Tony and team aren't even content there. His latest project involves transforming an entire city with his Downtown Project. This is serious big-picture thinking.

The notion of partnership really thrives at the Transcending level.

It seems to fly in the face of competition, but there's more to be had from "co-opetition" than wanting to destroy your competitors.

John Mackey, Co-CEO of Whole Foods, and Raj Sisodia, from their book, *Conscious Capitalism*, say it well:

"Imagine a business that views its competitors not as enemies to be crushed but as teachers to learn from and fellow travelers on the journey towards excellence."

Where I started in the online space, the most forward-thinking individuals were always looking at smart ways to partner up and provide value to each other's subscribers and lists. And for Evolved Enterprises, they care more about the mission being accomplished, so anyone else making a difference is welcomed in as a collaborator.

Networks Formed

What's more, at this level, partnerships are formed through coalitions and groups that help each other raise the bar. The outdoor apparel and lifestyle company Patagonia helped spearhead **"1% for the Planet,"** which now encompasses over 1,400 other companies donating 1% of their gross (not net) revenue to environmental causes of their choice.

Transcending is about gaining the elevation you need to discover the meaningful interconnections. Bruce Poon Tip, founder of G Adventures, with 1,500+ employees, is one of the world's most successful travel outfitters. In his book, *Looptail*, he talks about creating a movement beyond just a travel company, declaring that "you have to do what other companies are scared to do—you have to stand for something."

The looptail is finding your passion and purpose in your work and in your company, transcending your industry, and paying it forward. G Adventures has taken their primary asset and distribution channel consisting of thousands of travelers to leverage a greater shared impact.

For example, in Peru, they are one of the largest operators on the Inca Trail; they have tens of thousands of travelers per year. Through their Planeterra non-profit, they developed a women's weaving co-op. The travelers visit the co-op to learn how to weave, meet the locals, and, of course, buy their woven products. This is a true experience with a tremendous impact that drives revenue and raving fans.

I love this because everyone wins!

The traveler gets a better story to tell, they know they've made a difference, and the weavers actually interact in a meaningful way with customers to share their culture, provide a unique value, and ethically thrive.

Or take Salesforce as another example. They've built a **1-1-1 Philanthropic Model** based on a simple idea: leverage their technology, people, and resources to improve communities throughout the world. They call it the 1-1-1 model because they pledge 1% of profits, 1% of their time/talent, and 1% of their product. Marc Benioff, Chairman & CEO of Salesforce, has been quoted as saying, "The business of business is improving the state of the world."

Since their founding, they've given more than $128+ million in grants, given 1.6 million hours of community service, and provided product donations for more than 29,000 nonprofits and higher education institutions. And now they've taken this model and expanded it to include other companies to do the same with their **Pledge 1%** collective initiative. It encourages and challenges founders and companies to pledge 1% of equity, product, and employee time to causes of their choosing. And so far, 1,000 companies in 30 countries have taken the pledge, including Twilio, Glassdoor, Box, Yelp, General Assembly, Docusign, Salesforce, Atlassian, and Techstars.

In 2011 Harvard Business School professor Michael Porter wrote in the *Harvard Business Review*, "Businesses must reconnect company success with social progress. Shared value is not social responsibility, philanthropy, or even sustainability, but a new way to achieve economic success. It is not on the margin of what companies do but at the center."

My friend Jeff Cherry, one of the drivers of the Conscious Capitalism movement and founder of Conscious Ventures Labs in Maryland, says, "In the future, what a company stands for and 'how' it practices capitalism will determine future success." I agree. Jeff has a solid pedigree as part of the team that drilled down into the financial data for Firms of Endearment. He's got a background in finance and investment, so this is someone looking at the significant marketplace potential for Evolved Enterprises that gets this. I've been a mentor of companies coming out of the lab; they're raising a $50MM fund in this space, so it's not too hard to notice a shift is happening.

At the transcending level, we truly move into an entrepreneurial art form. You're using your business to creatively bring everything together in an elegant business model with an exponential impact for anyone your company interacts with. My dream for you is to...

Write the business "Love Story" you want the world to buy.

Let's take a look at some of the Evolved Enterprise Impact models and real-world examples that are working to actually make everything you do both alluring and attention getting...

CHAPTER THREE

11 EVOLVED ENTERPRISE IMPACT BUSINESS MODELS

I know when I see examples, things just 'click'...

And seeing these different models will get you totally excited about applying the Evolved Enterprise™ framework and ideas to anything you're doing.

When considering adding any of these elements or models of the Evolved Enterprise, it's important to consider something not really talked about in business.

And that is the "soul" of your company.

Huh?

By law, a corporation is its own entity, right? And as an entity, AKA a "body," the analogy follows that there is a soul inside. It can stand for something more. And just like we evolve, your business' purpose can evolve too.

A business could be created with the purpose of simply maximizing bottom line profit, or it could be exponentially expanded by having a distinctive mission or big "WHY." In the Evolved Enterprise model, these two do NOT have to be mutually exclusive.

I've categorized 11 models—but in many cases, a combination of several really works synergistically.

Evolved Enterprise Impact Model #1:
Buy One Give One (B1G1)

One of the biggest and most well-known examples is easily TOMS.

They've been a poster child for integrating and marrying impact with their business via their trademarked "one for one" model. TOMS has taken this and really run with it.

The story of TOMs shoes started when the founder, Blake Mycocskie, had a flash of an idea on a polo trip to Argentina. In his inspirational book, *Start Something That Matters*, Blake traces his humble beginnings to seeing firsthand kids going shoeless, and he wanted to make a change. And that notion of "every pair of shoes provides a pair for a child in need" became one of the biggest factors to their growth. It was an easy story consumers could spread. (That's actually key as we'll look at later on in story selling.) Another side benefit TOMS had when they started was the distinct look to their shoes—so other customers could identify fellow in-kind supporters. (We'll hit on this in Community Code 2.0.).

Blake says he never expected to grow so big, but they came in a perfect inflection point, where bigger companies were eager to partner with brands that had/have a social mission component and consumers were really aware of where their spending was going. Another powerful accelerator is partnering up with big companies that have massive reach and distribution. That's another big benefit from being an Evolved Enterprise; you'll get deals and joint ventures with companies that want to be associated with you for the "halo effect."

Forbes has confirmed their valuation at $625 million, with Bain Capital recently buying a 50% stake in the company. Not bad for a guy who only started selling his canvas footwear a few years ago.

TOMS started in shoes but has branched out to other products that support communities around the world. Their line of eyewear restores sight to an individual through sight-saving surgery, prescription glasses, or medical treatment. And then, just this year, they've launched TOMS Roasting Co. With every bag of coffee purchased, TOMS provides one week of clean water to a person in need.

The Buy One Give One (B1G1) model has been used in all sorts of products—everything from B1G1 programs like the "1 laptop per child" or the 1 Futbol project, with over 1.5M balls being distributed thanks to Chevy being a significant corporate partner.

TOMS didn't come up with the B1G1 model, but they've certainly got a lot of credit for it—so much so that I normally recommend Evolved Enterprises look to other models if it makes sense on a deeper level for their business. To just default to a B1G1 doesn't give you as big of a marketplace boost anymore, because that story has already been told. Plus, the model has been criticized for enabling a "handout" mentality. To some extent I agree; however, I also think critics just prefer to be critics, and the amount of good companies like TOMS have done is significant. I applaud anyone making a difference, and Blake has said one of the hardest things about being so big is actually the giving.

Instead of battling the criticism, TOMS has used this controversy to fuel solutions for how they can improve. Now they've moved 40% of their supply chain for giving shoes to countries that they give in. Today shoes are made in Kenya, India, Ethiopia, and Haiti.

In the true spirit of becoming a transcending business, TOMS is looking at ways to expand the reach of other Evolved Enterprises.

At one point, they created a marketplace platform that other Evolved Enterprises could be a part of to benefit from their mass distribution and leverage. TOMS was able to use their loyal customers, goodwill, brand reputation, and distribution to introduce other companies doing something important. This was one big step toward TOMS looking at ways to truly transcend business, and now they've stepped it up even more through their Social Enterprise Fund (toms.com/social-enterprise). Part of the arrangement with Bain Capital was also creating a fund and developing resources for "investing in the next generation of entrepreneurs using business to improve lives." It's a great way of continuing to use their talent, distribution, and reach to spread the idea of for-profit businesses that can make a difference.

Using These Exact Same Evolved Enterprise Principles, You Can Even Disrupt Major Monopolies That Have a Stranglehold on Their Marketplace

Who in their right mind would go after a market where one major player had 60–80% of the market in the U.S. alone? If you're eyewear company **Warby Parker** (WarbyParker.com), that's a recipe for disruption.

Warby Parker was founded in 2010 by four friends—Neil Blumenthal, Dave Gilboa, Andy Hunt, and Jeff Raider—who met at business school. By circumventing traditional channels, bypassing retail, designing glasses in-house, and engaging with customers directly, they were able to provide eyewear at a fraction of the going price. And when they combined that with a partnership with non-profits like VisionSpring to ensure that for every pair of glasses sold, a pair is distributed to someone in need, it was a big-time winning combination.

The launch was so successful that the team hit their first-year sales targets in the first three weeks.

The company has gone on to sell more than 1,000,000 pairs of glasses using a direct-to-consumer approach online and undercutting the $500 designer eyewear price. Their 1M pair milestone was hit in June 2014, and the biggest driver is their B1G1 messaging of donating a pair of glasses to someone in need with each purchase. The company tallies up the number sold at the end of the month and then donates that amount to one of their partners providing the eyewear on the ground.

Today, a few short years into their venture, the *Wall Street Journal* reported the company is valued at over $1B from a recent investment they took in.

Wow!

But again, this is the power of an Evolved Enterprise. And even better, as one of my colleagues reported back to me, *"It's just a heck of a lot more fun to have a business that makes an impact."*

But don't worry if you can't imagine yourself as big as some of these previous examples—the Evolved Enterprise concepts work even better if you're just getting started too.

Take Bombas Socks for example...

The founders, David Heath and Randy Goldberg, saw a news release that stated socks were the No. 1 most requested clothing item at homeless shelters. The two of them took that as a personal challenge to make a difference by building a better sock and to donate one pair for every pair sold to a homeless shelter.

That little idea turned into $2M in sales in just over one year and continued to grow at an accelerated clip.

They estimated it would take 10 years to get to a gigantic goal of 1,000,000 pairs donated—but they shattered that figure by doing it 8.5 years sooner! As an Evolved Enterprise, they were able to significantly increase their success by developing a community of fans who cared about spreading their message of doing good—plus it helped attract celebrity investors and partners like Daymond John from TV's *Shark Tank*.

And as Bombas has grown, their culture of impact continues to be baked in. The founders and their staff, which is now up to 15, take one day a month to volunteer at a shelter, at a soup kitchen, or with one of their hundreds of giving partners.

I'd be totally remiss if I didn't mention this fun example. One of our previous Underground® presenters, Greg Clement, is a serial entrepreneur in multiple industries. One day his pastor's seven-year-old son came up with an idea for a blanket to sell and to give away to kids in hospitals. Being the business guy, Greg became the CEO and headed up the **"Happy Blankie" project** (Everythinghappy.com).

The core philosophy is "One to Love, One to Give®," and its mission is to donate blankies to children in need all over the world. They have made donations to orphanages and hospitals in Africa, Thailand, China, and Haiti as well as several hospitals and Ronald McDonald houses across the U.S. I love the way Greg and team have re-framed B1G1 with a bigger benefit of "one to love and one to give"—very smart. It looks like they've now expanded into licensed characters and other kids' accessories and clothing.

For Evolved Enterprises that want to tie into this B1G1 model, it's really worth checking out **B1G1.com**. The site is a platform for companies that connects them to 800+ opportunities for giving directly.

It makes it easy for companies to give to and support great projects from around the world. According to the site, they've already tracked over 80,000,000 "giving impacts" created by small businesses being part of B1G1 Business for Good worldwide.

I had the co-founder, Paul Dunn, come out recently to present to our Maverick members, and they were blown away by the flexibility and creativity that could be facilitated through the platform.

You can use it in numerous ways to grow your business with giving as a byproduct. The platform allows you to search by regions of the world you want to impact and/or categories of projects you prefer.

It works for so many types of companies with a little bit of imagination. For instance, if you're a professional services firm – think about the shock and amazement that would happen if you sent a certificate detailing the impact you've made on a client's behalf for the exact cause they care about? Paul shared the story of a financial planner doing exactly this as one poignant example. From their conversations she found out her client really cared about music. And after they signed on with the firm, she made a direct impact for providing music lessons and education to underprivileged youth in that client's name. You better believe they became a raving fan of the firm when they found out about this meaningful gesture.

One of the really exciting benefits of this platform is not tying into the dollar amount but the actual "giving impact," as they call it. From a quick search, I found inexpensive programs like providing breakfast for a job seeker in South Africa for $1.00 to as little as one penny for e-learning initiatives in India.

Note: Paul has graciously provided a $20 giving credit that will be credited in your account when you sign up. Use the code: **EVOLVED**. (Just go to **B1G1.com**, and then the code field is found when you're on the membership registration page.)

Evolved Enterprise Impact Model #2: Direct Impact

Specificity sells, and showing where you are making a direct impact really works.

One company that really does this well is **FEED** (feedprojects.com). They started with a simple concept: buy one bag and feed one child for a year in a developing country. Boom! Simple idea combined with an outwardly physical symbol (the bag), and you've got a winning combination.

After witnessing the effects of hunger firsthand, Lauren Bush founded FEED in 2007 with the mission of "Creating Good Products That Help FEED the World."

She first created the FEED 1 Bag, a reversible burlap and organic cotton bag. It was stamped with "FEED the children of the world" and the number "1" to signify that each bag provides enough meals to feed one child in school for one year. To date, the business has been able to provide nearly 84 million meals globally.

I love the idea of creating something (that's wanted) with a byproduct for good (e.g., buy a fashionable bag and feed "x" number of children). The bag is very prominently printed with the word FEED on it, and it gives the buyer/donor an identity as someone who makes a difference with their purchases.

What's more, they have one of the most innovative Impact Score-boards I've seen:

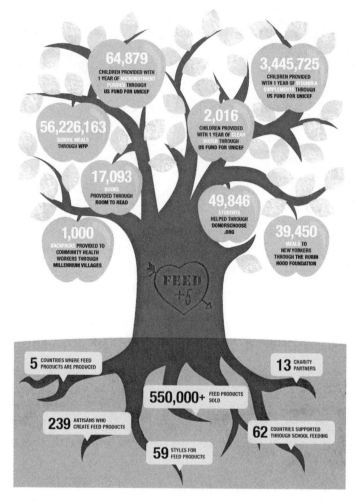

One of the pitfalls of a direct impact is making sure there is an authentic and understandable tie-in. You want your customers and fans to fully see the connection to what you're doing in order to spread your marketing message for you.

I recently bought a new watch as a fun fashion accessory. It came in all sorts of cool colors with interchangeable bands. I stumbled on the site right before going on our annual Maverick Impact trip to Haiti, and this company provided water filters in Haiti for each watch sold. The natural tie-in is a bit hard to explain to anyone who comments on my awesome new watch. (Note: In the Creation and Community chapters, we'll discuss how to create artifacts that people want to talk about to spread your selling stories.)

Make no mistake, it's critical that the story is strong enough and easy enough to spread.

For instance, if I owned this watch company, I would create something around the idea of "time for change." Or maybe take it one step further and create specific times, like 4:44 GMT, where everyone who is wearing this watch is reminded to think/imagine/visualize/meditate on global peace.

I'm just kind of shooting from the hip here—but can't you see how much more powerful that is for a watch brand? It builds community and does truly transcend business. Sure, it still has some direct impact toward an organization that promotes peace. When there's an authentic tie-in in every way, it gets so much more interesting. Maybe there's even a built-in alarm (set to go off by default) for that time that reminds the wearers. I've seen studies of people coming together to meditate on peace that have shown a reduction in crime rates in cities, so maybe this isn't so far fetched; someone might take this ideas and run with it.

I love it when there is a smart tie-in. Check out LSTN **Sound Co.** (http://lstnsound.co). They sell very nicely designed, real-wood headphones, ear buds, and speakers. Their mission was to create a company that could create global change by providing high-quality products that help fund hearing restoration and spread awareness for the global problem of hearing loss and hearing impairment.

With each purchase, there is a direct impact to provide hearing aids to a person in need through their charity partner, Starkey Hearing Foundation. In under three years, LSTN has been able to help give the gift of sound to over 20,000 people.

I've been fortunate to volunteer with Starkey twice now in Africa, and these hearing aid missions are absolutely life changing. After a bit of instruction and a little hand-holding, you are pretty much on our own while fitting hearing aids. And there's nothing more rewarding than being able to immediately and instantly impact someone's life with the gift of hearing. I remember fitting one remarkable grandmother in South Africa who was brought in by her granddaughter. She told us her grandmother had never heard since her granddaughter was born, and I would have estimated the granddaughter's age at approximately 25–30. You actually get an immediate reaction when you find the right amplification, and I remember staring into this woman's cataract-wizened eyes and seeing them pop wide open. She had heard for the first time in decades, and we both cried.

Evolved Enterprise Impact Model #3: Percentage or Dollar Amount

Probably one of the most used ways for companies to make a difference is committing to a percentage or certain dollar amount donated to a cause or charity.

I've got some more empirical proof that you make more when you give more. One of my colleagues, Brett Fogle, launched a new Forex trading course, and he had decided to split test this certificate on his sales page. They tested with the certificate and without. But having the page with the certificate raised the conversion by 10%. Now, this was a $2,000 product, and the 10% bump helped them write a $40,000.00 charity check.

Very exciting because that ten percent bump also represented tens of thousands in additional sales that wouldn't have happened without this tie-in.

Developing a percent or specific dollar amount from the product works—but let's take this a step further. As an Evolved Enterprise, you can create an even more integrated way of making this more impactful.

Sevenly (Sevenly.org) is a company really exploding because of their integrated impact. We had the co-founder, Dale Partridge, present to Maverick1000 members on how their growth came up with a compelling "built-in" story customers wanted to share. Dale told our group it's because 80% of their new buyers come from social media shares. This is huge! **That means you re-allocate funding that might normally go into a marketing budget and move into making a meaningful difference.**

What started as just one t-shirt design per week has now grown to several other pieces of clothing and accessories. And you can see the power of their growing story selling because Sevenly has actually donated over $4,400,000 in a few years and is growing rapidly.

The concept started simply for the direct impact—they would donate $7 per featured purchase per week toward the featured cause as part of seven main areas of help. Get it? Hence the name, the donation amount, and the length of time to accumulate the donation. (They've since updated their model to 7% on purchases.)

They do an incredible job of harnessing their community and fans to help accelerate and spread their marketing message. Plus, it's making a direct difference that can be counted. Here's a recent snapshot showing their Impact Scoreboard:

Total Raised
$3,835,783

People Helped
1,363,512

Total Shares
298,440

Because each cause they work with has a direct impact, they can show how many lives they've changed. I love the transparency and specificity here.

At Maverick, we use this same model, with members automatically contributing 10% of their dues to our Impact Fund. We use this fund to help entrepreneurial non-profit and cause partners develop real-world solutions to their pressing problems. Part of the fund is then allocated to actually implementing the solution we've jointly created. I'm always thinking about how we can create a ripple effect with the amount accumulated. One of the experiments we're starting to do is actually taking a global cause (i.e., the declining number of bees) and working together with young entrepreneurs to develop self-sustaining, for-profit businesses to help there. The Impact Fund is used as prize money to get those ventures started. This way it's not just a donation but seed capital for something bigger.

Evolved Enterprise Impact Model #4a: Donate What You Want

This model is really interesting because you give consumers the power and choice of paying and/or donating what they want. **Humble Bundle** has really blown up on this model.

Humble Bundles are digital packages of software or games available for a limited time (i.e., two weeks). These have been ultra successful, with several bundles generating over $1M in revenue. According to Wikipedia, numbers in August 2013 put the bundles at over $50M in total sales and $20M in charity donations.

I've also seen a few restaurants, and even Panera Bread, experimenting with not having a fixed price for their menus.

Evolved Enterprise Impact Model #4b: Donate Where You Want

The impact changes based on the product line bought. For instance, **Project7** (Project7.com), founded by Tyler Merrick in 2008, lets consumers decide on which of the seven causes they support depending on the flavor of gum or mints they buy. The seven causes chosen by Project 7 are the areas where they see the most need in this world. As they say, "Feeding the Hungry, Healing the Sick, supporting those who Hope for Peace, Housing the Homeless, Quenching Those Who Thirst, Teaching Them Well, and Saving the Earth." And these little purchases can add up for everyday items bought. They've done a great job of ensuring their product packaging has their Impact Scoreboard prominently showcased with their total contributions made.

1 Face Watch company (1face.com) sells fun and fashionable watches in all sorts of bright colors. The only difference is each color represents a different cause and a different direct impact. For instance, there's the yellow watch supporting pencils of promise with five watches sold equaling a year of education. Or you can get the white watch supporting cause partner Faces of Change, which develops rural food programs. One watch = feeding 10 people. Essentially, the buyer can pick their favorite trendy color or make a purchase based on the direct impact they want to make. At $40 per watch, you might even pick up several. If you're in a certain age group, you might remember back in the day wearing two or three Swatches at once, so maybe this will catch on again. ;)

Evolved Enterprise Impact Model #5: "All In"

Newman's Own is the king of this model, from humble origins in 1982 with a homemade salad dressing outlined in the book *Shameless Exploitation in Pursuit of the Common Good*, written by the famous actor and his co-founder, A.E. Hotchne. The brand, even after Paul's passing, has grown into a mega food empire, and it had given over $300MM by 2010. The business model is to give away all profits to organizations aligned with the company's values. They started with funding camps for seriously ill children and have expanded. Of course, it doesn't hurt to have some Hollywood glitz sprinkled with Paul dressed up in funny outfits for each product. But there's no denying the level of impact they've had.

Greyston Bakery's (greyston.com) philosophy is *"We don't hire people to bake brownies, we bake brownies to hire people."* What originally began as a modest bakery has grown into a broad array of programs supporting the community. With over $11MM in revenue, one of the keystones has been Greyston's aims to hire the hard-to-employ and "open hiring" practices, where anyone can sign up regardless of background. All profits from the company go to the Greyston Foundation, which uses it for low-income housing, day care open to the community, a medical center for those with AIDS, and other community endeavors.

These models are not just for consumer-facing companies. **Impact Makers** (impactmakers.com) is a management and technology consulting company based in Richmond, Virginia. They are a for-profit company that has gifted its ownership to the community and contributes 100% of its net profits to charities over the life of the company.

This unique aspect has helped them make the Inc. 5000 List of Fastest Growing Private Companies in America for five consecutive years. In 2015, they contributed more than $450,000 in direct, unrestricted financial support and pro bono management and tech consulting to their partner charities.

I want to be really clear here: All profits does NOT mean this is a non-profit venture (nor should it be).

In fact, Impact Makers is clear on this in their FAQs:

Impact Makers operates as any for-profit firm in that it seeks to maximize revenue and minimize expenditures. As such, it can attract top talent by compensating its staff and consultants at market rates. However, unlike a traditional for-profit firm, Impact Makers gives 100 percent of its net profits to charities over the life of the company, after paying salaries, operating expenses, and taxes.

I worry about a "no profits" model for entrepreneurs that come to business with a deep desire for impact without considering the financial side. They have a mistaken idea that they should put every cent into the cause, almost like the "starving artist" misconception.

Perhaps this has come from the values portrayed in the media or popular culture about the "filthy rich" or the notion that you've screwed someone in some way—or even misunderstood dogmas about the virtues of poverty. That couldn't be more incorrect. **Business relies on providing value in exchange for the consumer's money.** The buyer is not coerced or forced into making a purchase.

A perfect illustration of this showed up at a recent Family Freedom entrepreneurial event we put on. The event is about teaching business ideas to kids and actually getting them out on the streets to figure it out themselves (Maverick1000.com/family). At one of the 4th of July events, the children divided up into teams selling all sorts of light-up bracelets and patriotic products.

Each team is responsible for knowing their margins and costs plus figuring out their promotional and selling tactics. One team got the idea that all the money would go to support the local fire department in Park City, UT. There had been a lot of wild fires raging when we were there, and it made it an easy decision. They even arranged to get full fire coats and boots for the kids to sell the glow sticks for donations. Their "sales" totaled approximately $1,800, I believe, with the next closest team at $150–200. But while they technically made more, they didn't keep it. After paying the hard costs back to "Mr. Yanik," they then donated everything left to the fire department.

This led to a good discussion at our debrief about what would happen now that they had zero capital to buy more inventory, advertise, etc. By giving away every cent without any thought to compensation and other expenses, it leaves the company vulnerable to going out of business and then creating zero impact!

I have absolutely no qualms with founders and key team members being paid exceptional profits but only if they are providing exceptional value. This is also a balancing act of what dollars or percentage are contributed to the impact side of the equation.

Evolved Enterprise Impact Model #6: Source Matters

I've been impressed with so many clothing and food companies looking back at exactly where their supply chain comes from and the impact along the way. They've certainly led the field here with this impact model.

For instance, Yvon Choinard, the founder of **Patagonia**, has always been about putting the environment first—even before their company. (I actually think this has only helped their sales and fan base since consumers can spot inauthentic values.)

Over the past 40 years, Patagonia has consistently done the unusual, from looking at how to only use ethical raw material to even telling consumers to purchase less of their products with a recent Black Friday full-page ad.

In 1996 they switched from conventional to organic cotton. It raised their raw material costs by 3X, but they did it because it was less harmful to the environment. As a private company with sales over $400MM, Choinard is passionate about showing small and big companies how to do business in a different way. According to the founder, "I hang onto Patagonia because it's my resource to do something good. It's a way to demonstrate that corporations can lead examined lives."

And in line with the Transcending level of business, they've formed a Sustainable Apparel Coalition with some unlikely partners, like Walmart and Levi's. However, they come together for a positive ROI because the members with bigger footprints have the ability to make small changes that have a tremendous impact and bottom line results by looking at their supply chain. According to a recent *Wall Street Journal* article, when Walmart worked with Choinard, they actually saved money through environmental initiatives, like reducing its packaging and water consumption. And that's the secret. There has to be (and there already is) a real economic incentive to make a difference.

Transparency

Patagonia also was one of the first to provide transparency with their Footprint Chronicles detailing 100% of what goes into their products (patagonia.com/us/footprint).

In a similar vein, one of my other favorite gear companies is **Icebreaker**, taking transparency to another level. I pretty much live in Icebreaker clothing, including my undies that I'm wearing right now. (TMI?)

Icebreaker makes all their clothing from merino wool because of the softness, durability, and low odor absorption, among other characteristics. They even went so far as to let you trace back your item to the source...the sheep. There was a "Baa Code" on the clothing to "check the living conditions of the sheep, meet the growers who raised them, and follow the production process through to the finished garment," according to the site.

I admit I haven't checked in on the sheep used for my gear—but just simply having that code provides me with the peace of mind that there is care and forethought with the source.

HailMerry, a producer of delicious raw food goodies, creates transparency in an elegant way on their packaging with these five elegant words before listing what's inside: "We celebrate our pure ingredients." Perfect.

Dr. Bronner's Magic Soap has quite an eccentric and colorful story of being an Evolved Enterprise pioneer for decades (drbronner.com/our-story/timeline/). Founded by Emmanuel Bronner, a third-generation soap maker from Germany, the company started serendipitously because Bronner would provide free peppermint soap to attendees of his lectures on world peace. It became more evident people were attending for the soap, so Bronner sold the soap and started printing his talks on the bottles.

When an organic fair trade source for their ingredient oils couldn't be located, they simply started their own. They created their own organic and fair-trade palm, coconut, and olive farms in Ghana, Sri Lanka, and Israel. To be in alignment with their vision of world peace, the olive oil is sourced from both Israel and Palestine.

Fairphone (fairphone.com) started as an awareness campaign in 2010 and then grew into a full-pledged company selling phones with a big mission. As they say on the site, "The stuff that goes into your phone has an impact on people and the planet. We want to go straight to the source to make sure we're creating positive change."

Fairphone provides radical transparency, showing where the rare materials and minerals for their phone come from to ensure conflict-free mining. Conflicts include funding rebel groups, neglecting workers' rights, safety and the ability to earn fair wages, and political and economic instability. They even go so far as to make their business model transparent by showing how much each margin is in every product purchase and what it costs to run the enterprise, from developing products and social projects to manufacturing, marketing, and operations. (www.fairphone.com/en/our-goals/how-we-work/fairphone-cost-breakdown/)

Even much smaller companies can consider this model. **Teakoe** is an artisan tea company from Colorado and is a good example of a company taking into consideration sustainability in what they are doing. On their page about sustainability (teakoe.com/pages/sustainability), they reveal exactly how they focus on making their environment better by operating this way. Teakoe made their packaging and teas compostable and packing eco-friendly—but they've considered other factors beyond their core components too. They look at manufacturing, recycling, waste byproducts, low emission delivery vehicles, and setting responsible business practices.

Repurposing on Purpose

Taking raw or discarded material and finding a better use that creates an impact is how this model works. Apparel and accessory companies lead the way here, but I can see other industries being sparked by these ideas too. This model works because it has a built-in cost savings for discarded materials being reused and a massive savings to the environment. Plus, there is a creative element to elevate a raw material into a higher and better use.

One of my favorite Evolved Enterprise companies applying this Impact model is **Elvis and Kresse**. The idea started when the founders saw abandoned fire hoses on the road that would be headed for the landfill. These two designers thought it was a beautiful material to work with and have now created bags, shower kits, wallets, belts, etc., from the hose.

Elvis & Kresse redistributes up to 50% of profits to projects and charities related to the unique materials they reclaim. Fifty percent of the profits from their fire hose range are donated to the Fire Fighters Charity. Here's what they say on their site:

> *Why do we make these donations? At Elvis & Kresse, we believe in the notion of good business: our business was established to solve environmental problems, waste problems in particular. We started with fire hose and now reclaim more than 10 different materials. Beyond this, we also wanted to engage our material partners, our key stakeholders. Why not share, and why not see if more good could be done with the surplus of an already good business? Why not?*
>
> *In this sense, we are lucky. Most traditional businesses are only able to measure their success in one way—the bottom line. At Elvis & Kresse, we have two additional measures of success: how much*

waste we are able to divert from landfills and how much money
we are able to give back to our charities, of which all three have
equal importance to us.

What makes this intriguing to me is that the material itself is in total
authentic alignment to the way their impact is created.

Refresh Glass (refreshglass.com) takes "rescued"
wine bottles and converts them into drinkware
and home décor. The company collects empty
wine bottles from local Arizona restaurants and
hotels that would have otherwise thrown them
away. They then transform them into beautiful glassware. I have a set in our house that I
received as a gift, and they're great.

They have a mission to recover 10,000,000 wine bottles and are
approaching 1M right now. According to the site, one rescued wine
bottle saves enough energy to light a 100-watt light bulb for four hours,
power a computer for 30 minutes, or power a television for 20 minutes.

Sword & Plough (swordandplough.com) could potentially hit a few
of our categories. They consistently repurpose military surplus such
as tents, sleeping bag covers, uniform fabric, military spec canvas and
nylon, and any other materials to turn them into bags, accessories, and
articles of clothing. There's a full-circle impact aspect to supporting
veterans at every stage (from product conception to order fulfillment).
That includes working with American manufacturers that employ veterans and donating 10% of profits back to veteran organizations.

+Income Opportunities

Not only are there recycling opportunities with this model to alle-
viate waste but also potential income opportunities for different

communities to collect the refuse.

From the projects I participate in Haiti, I've come across a few pretty remarkable companies sourcing recycled plastic to create jobs and economic opportunities.

Thread (threadinternational.com) is supplying fabric that is converted from water bottles and other plastic trash to clothing manufacturers. They meticulously track the impact on job creation in Haiti and Honduras and the positive environmental effect from removing the trash. But even though the product is better, they still need to sell it in a way that's a benefit to clothing manufacturers that are more inclined to pay the lowest price for raw materials unless there really is a difference.

Thread had to get good at highlighting those benefits for partners— everything from research on increased customer loyalty (improved brand sentiment by 12.5%) to increased PR ($300 of earned media per yard of fabric). Ian Rosenberger, CEO of Thread, is also thinking about the human element to introduce his customers to the people whose lives are changed in their supply chain. This makes the social and economic impact real. What's more, they provide bigger brands the exact pre-done story kits they need to share their impact story with their end user consumers.

Another project that looks at waste as a vehicle to improve lives is **Plastic Bank** (plasticbank.org). Plastic Bank was piloted in Peru a few years back and is now being introduced in Haiti. The big idea is to have the public collect plastic bottles that are then crushed into pellets to be sold. The business model is to provide a financial incentive for collecting these bottles from cash, access to Wi-Fi, or access to power to charge their mobile phones.

Evolved Enterprise Impact Model #7:
Experience the Good

Charity auctions and fundraisers have been a staple of donation efforts for non-profits, but a new group of companies has come mixing this with celebrity firepower. **Charity Buzz** (charitybuzz.com) is an online auction marketplace where you can bid on unique experiences. Charity Buzz keeps 20% of the auction price and gives 80% back to the charity. The organization is doing big things with a milestone of over $100MM raised for different charities since its inception in 2005.

In a similar vein, there's **If Only** (ifonly.com), which also provides unique experiences with celebrity chefs, tastemakers, and luminaries. They operate as an auction program or a fixed price.

A really interesting entry in this category is **Omaze** (omaze.com). They work a little bit like a sweepstakes, where they put up really intriguing experiences to benefit charities, like riding around in a real tank with Arnold Schwarzenegger and smashing things. The interesting twist they've added is a viral component to give you more chances to win, and they allow you to purchase multiple packages of entries with better rewards attached to them.

For instance, for a recent experience with comedian Seth Rogen, you could purchase entries from $10 to $25,000, guaranteeing a sit-down lunch with Seth. Their split with the charity is a similar 80/20.

Now the experiences don't have to only be auctioned off. Consider this example from Carnival Corp. Yes, I'm talking about the $16-billion-per year cruising giant that is dipping both feet in with **Fathom** (fathom. org). Described as "Impact Travel," Fathom's dedicated ship will send passengers on volunteer missions to the Dominican Republic and Cuba, where they will work with local charities. This is the only thing the cruise will offer, and the programming will be dedicated to the "voluntourism" effort. No doubt Carnival is looking at Fathom as a strategic way to counter some of the poor press from their environmental impact and to counter the trend of cruising not appealing to millennials. But even with that said, I do believe they can make an impact.

Evolved Enterprise Impact Model #8: Empowered Employment

This model is called Empowered Employment because the companies work directly with underserved or marginalized communities for labor, creation, and design. But it's not simply a "feel-good" aspect of the business, because when integrated creatively, it actually produces a value-driven differentiator.

Some of these examples to learn from are a mix of for-profit and non-profits.

Founded in 2008 by Leila Janah, **Samasource** (sama-source.org) uses the model of digital outsourcing to address poverty by redirecting a small part of the $200B+ spent on outsourcing to poor women and youth in developing countries. Samasource estimates 43 million people could benefit from the Microwork™ model, which transforms complex data projects into small, computer-based tasks. This work helps women and youth build skills and generate life-changing income.

Being pragmatic here, the work has to be on par and on budget with what these clients could contract in other ways. But if that's the case, then the "halo effect" is huge here and makes it an easy decision to work with Samasource.

And when there's alignment around something bigger, the Universe seems to conspire to come together in our favor. These are moments that Carl Jung would label synchronicity that have significant meaning well beyond coincidence.

Actress and singer/songwriter Caitlin Crosby, founder of **The Giving Keys**, might agree. She would wear an old NYC key around her neck engraved with inspirational words. On tours, she'd sell an assortment of keys with messages like "hope," "strength," "believe," etc. Every night the keys would sell out, and she started to encourage people to give their necklace to someone they felt needed the message on that particular key. Now the keys were creating stories and connection shared on thegivingkeys.com site.

The notion of a conscious business really clicked one night when she saw a couple on Hollywood Blvd. sitting under an umbrella and holding a sign that read, "Ugly, Broke & Hungry." They went to dinner, and Caitlin discovered that Cera made jewelry, which was exactly what she needed. Rob and Cera joined the team and started making Giving Keys the next day.

Today, the Giving Keys employs those who are looking for a transition out of homelessness. They've partnered with the United Way and PATH, a reputable transitional home in LA. This combination makes an Evolved Enterprise™ powerfully compelling to consumers and partners. Today, the Giving Keys are carried in over 500 stores in the U.S. and internationally, including Anthropologie, Fred Segal, Henri Bendel, and Kitson.

Mirakle Couriers in India is another exceptional example of a transcending level Evolved Enterprise worth spotlighting. Mirakle Couriers' business model is based on creating a service-driven, profitable enterprise that utilizes the deaf. In India, anyone with a disability is typically discriminated against, and there is severe lack of government support for the deaf population. Mirakle Couriers was born when founder Dhruv Lakra focused on a courier business because it requires a lot of visual skills but no verbal communication. Fact is, the deaf are extremely good at map reading and remembering roads and buildings because they are so visually inclined. With each package delivered, the couriers also provide an educational sheet educating their customers about being deaf and how they can help. Again, this is a total win/win/win across the board.

In a similar fashion, **Signs Restaurant** in Canada (signsrestaurant.ca) hires deaf servers and hopes to help create a dialogue between those with hearing difficulties and the non-deaf people eating here. All the menus come with ASL cheat sheets to help everyone communicate and experience a shared bond. It's an engaging concept that can make a difference.

Another wonderfully inspiring example of this model is **Sarah Oliver Handbags** (saraoliverhandbags). The story goes that Sarah started designing handbags as gifts for friends and family. The bags received were so popular that she began selling them at trunk shows, and retail stores began to call. She didn't want to manufacture overseas, so she decided on a novel approach recruiting residents of a local senior retirement community to hand knit the bags. This team of knitters, with an average age of 88, have named themselves the Purlettes +1. They are aptly named for their "knit one, purl two" expertise as well as the pearls of wisdom they impart. The + 1 represents the sole male knitter, Hector.

I love this because it gives seniors purpose and honors their skills for something remarkable. (Plus, notice how they are given a name/identity: "Purlettes." We'll cover this more in the Community chapter.)

ULTRA Testing (ultratesting.us) takes this concept of empowered employment one step further. Founded in 2012 by a pair of former MIT roommates on the premise that "disability" can be a source of competitive advantage, ULTRA's first service delivers high-quality software testing by employing onshore teams of individuals with Autism

Spectrum Disorders.

There are 1.5 million Americans on the autism spectrum, and they're usually at a disadvantage in traditional office environments. But not everywhere. People with autism and Asperger's tend to engage in repetitive behaviors that others might consider boring, which allows them to maintain focus as they test whether a given piece of software works on different devices, operating systems, and web browsers over, and over, and over again—a significant advantage and perfect match for the work they are doing.

Several non-profits have taken the lead here as well with empowered employment development.

For nearly 30 years now, **Homeboy Industries** has been serving high-risk, formerly gang-involved men and women with a continuum of free services and programs and operates seven social enterprises that serve as job-training sites for their "boys" and "girls."

Today Homeboy Industries spans printing, groceries, baked goods, diners, and apparel. Plus, they even have licensed products with Ralph's supermarkets and a licensed Homeboy diner at the LAX airport.

A significant pioneer of this model is **Delancey Street** (Delancey-streetfoundation.org), with revenues topping $24MM between the interconnected companies. Founded in 1991 by Mimi Halper Silbert with just four residents, a $1,000 loan, and a dream to create a new model to help people out of substance abuse and employ former felons, Dr. Silbert has received national and international attention for her achievement at Delancey Street, where she demonstrates her belief that the people who are the problem can become the solution.

Delancey successfully operates everything from food and hospitality businesses, such as cafes and catering, to small manufacturing firms building handcrafted furniture and ironworks, to service-based enterprises providing car services, printing, landscaping, and moving.

The average resident has been a hard-core drug and alcohol abuser, has been in prison, is unskilled, is functionally illiterate, and has a personal history of violence and generations of poverty. The minimum stay at Delancey Street is two years, while the average resident remains for almost four years—drug-, alcohol-, and crime-free. During their time at Delancey Street, residents receive a GED and are trained in three different marketable skills.

Another excellent example we've worked with is **Opportunity Village** (opportunityvillage.org), heralded as one of Las Vegas' most impactful organizations. They are a conglomerate of business services and ventures working with people with intellectual disabilities. Not only do they provide skill training for employment but they also run their own business units internally. These range from package inserts, shredding, document imaging, button creation, wholesale baking, and more. One of my favorite programs the Maverick members saw behind the scenes were their creative ventures, with participants selling their artwork and keeping 50% of the profits.

Think of your significant competitive advantage here with the teams of empowered employees having a bigger and much deeper meaning at work. The degree of loyalty and full engagement here is at a totally different level.

Evolved Enterprise Impact Model #9: Co-Development

This model directly connects the producers and buyers to create an even better experience and impact for everyone involved.

Take a look at **Good Eggs** (goodeggs.com). They position themselves like a grocery store but better since you order online directly from farmers and food makers for delivery of the freshest foods. It works for everyone. The model is great for producers since they know exactly how much to make to reduce waste and spoilage. And it works for consumers too since they get only the freshest and most in-season produce. Good Eggs is only in a few cities right now but hopefully will be expanding.

Aid Through Trade (aidthroughtrade.com) was started in 1993 by a former Peace Corps volunteer. It is now one of the leaders in the fair trade fashion industry and employs over 75 women artisans in Nepal to create jewelry from high-quality glass beads. Aid Through Trade connects these jewelry designers to consumers in the West and, in turn, provides fair trade business practices for their employees—everything from fair pay to additional benefits such as retirement and healthcare benefits that usually are not available.

I-DEV International is a New York–based impact investment firm that develops industries in emerging countries. In Peru, they helped farmers build an international business out of tara, a native tree species whose fruit had historically been consumed locally. After finding new applications for tara in the global food, pharmaceutical, leather, and pet-food industries, 200 Peruvian farmers organized a co-op. This co-op generates nearly $7MM in revenue for members.

Tourism is the world's largest job creator, and **Open Africa** (openafrica.org) stimulates rural development by leveraging communities'

collective tourism assets. They work with small businesses to establish rural tourism routes that offer tourists authentic experiences while generating income and jobs for local people. Outfitters and authentic tourist destination experiences are connected to customers through Open Africa's marketing platforms.

Evolved Enterprise Impact Model #10: Ethical Opportunity

A little extra income, for most people, is absolutely life-changing. Now multiply that several times over for developing countries, where extra income is completely game changing. Impact model #10 piggybacks on already proven models of having reps distribute your products, creating a new breed of Evolved Enterprises.

If you look at direct sales goliaths like Avon or Amway, they are self-replicating masters with their business opportunity that allows reps to sell a full array of products.

Living Goods founder Chuck Slaughter, fresh from his success at mail order giant TravelSmith, looked at this model and thought it could be replicated to make a bigger impact. He wondered if the power of Avon's model of door-to-door agents could lower costs, grow profits, and improve rural reach. Living Goods franchises its brand and business model to women entrepreneurs who work as independent agents. To launch their Living Goods franchise, agents receive a microloan and an initial setup of inventory and business tools. The agents sell life-saving products like mosquito nets, medicine, water purification tablets, and more to rural villages where distribution for such products is sparse. It's a total win/win/win.

Starting in Uganda in 2008, there are now over 1,000 agents making a real difference and earning a real income for themselves. The company has just expanded into Kenya, and it's very exciting to watch because direct selling is one of the fastest-growing consumer models, especially in developing countries.

VisionSpring leverages direct agents and makes it work in a big way. They are targeting the Bottom of the Pyramid (BoP), with $3,000 or less in annual income, and representing 4B consumers. They are not looking at this group as needing handouts but rather as a viable market that can be activated through a high-volume and low-margin approach.

They employ a Hub-and-Spoke approach, where their optical shops function as hubs and vision entrepreneurs (their sales agents) act like spokes conducting outreach in the communities surrounding the optical shops. Each one supports and sustains the other. Vision entrepreneurs are local people that the organization has trained to conduct vision screenings and educate their communities about the importance of eye care and the benefits of corrected vision.

VisionSpring's vision stores generate income via programs in which higher profit margins on more expensive glasses subsidize basic eyewear for the poorest customers. They continue operating on a nonprofit basis while working toward profitability in every country where they operate. The El Salvador unit is already profitable, and they expect operations in India to achieve profitability by 2015.

Bigger companies have been experimenting with this direct sales model too. In Brazil, **Nestlé** is reaching BoP consumers in urban favelas through a network of micro-distributors and direct sales agents. The Nestlé Até Você model provides an opportunity for women from their local communities who have lived there for at least five years and have built up trust.

The MLM company, Mannatech, created a Mission 5 Million program a few years ago to link any consumer purchase to a donation of their nutritional supplementation. Since 2005 they have reported 98,000,000 servings donated to children in need.

The direct selling model has grown, with independent reps using their own social networks, and one of those growth areas is "party plan" selling. You've probably been invited to one of these or know about them. The most famous is Tupperware, but there are so many more. There is everything from jeans parties, candle parties, handbag parties, jewelry parties, toys and puzzles, skin care, and so much more. Nearly anything can be sold this way. I've yet to really see a company employ the Evolved Enterprise model with party selling, so this could be a tremendous untapped distribution channel.

There is a remarkable opportunity to combine an ethical "biz opp" for individuals to make a little bit of extra income (which is an almost universal want) with a good product that makes a difference.

Evolved Enterprise Impact Model #11: Ecosystem

A few years back one of the clients I coached said something I really liked: *"The more META you go, the more leverage there is."*

I've been really engaged thinking about the leverage available through the interconnected nature of an ecosystem. This is an advanced model but one that can work on so many different levels. My friend Ari Weinzweig, co-founder of Zingerman's, is fond of mentioning, *"The healthiest ecosystems are the most diverse and complex."*

He should know. Zingerman's is one of the companies I really admire for the unique way they've built an interconnected (kind of a vertically integrated) grouping of related businesses.

I had heard and read a bunch about Zingerman's approach to business and knew it was interesting and different...but didn't realize how unusual it really was until I dug in.

And the more I saw, the more I really loved how they built their business, the philosophy, the culture, and more. There's a reason *Inc* magazine referred to them as "the coolest business in America" in one of their issues.

Here's the backstory...

It all started as a simple deli in Ann Arbor, Michigan, in 1982 with co-founder Paul Saginaw. The notion was to give local residents real, authentic deli food and never skimp on the quality. Over the next decade, Zingerman's deli became a hit for their food but hit a plateau at about $5 million in revenue. It was at that point that they came up with an ingenious plan for creating growth without sacrificing the elements of being a small business in a community they loved. In fact, Ari was adamant that he would not expand Zingerman's deli to a bunch of other cities, attempt to duplicate the ambiance, and create some mediocre version of what they had started.

Interconnected Community of Businesses

Instead, in 1992 Ari and Paul wrote out their vision for 2004. It was to have a group of 10–12 small businesses, referred to as **Zingerman's Community of Businesses, or ZCoB**. And that's exactly what happened. Each one would bear the Zingerman's name but have their own unique identity and specialty—everything from a bakeshop to a mail order facility to a training and seminar company teaching the "secret sauce" to their success.

But that's only half the story because they sell to each other, creating a built-in customer base. For example, the bakery makes all the baked goods, breads, etc., for the deli and also sells wholesale to other retailers.

They use shared resources of IT, HR, PR, marketing, payroll, etc., running it as another division with each business unit paying in. I love immersing myself in their world while visiting for great food and new insight. I couldn't recommend getting up there more or at least picking

Ari's recent series of *Lapsed Anarchist's Approach* business books available at ZingTrain.com.

So what is an ecosystem?

Let's define an ecosystem from Wikipedia: http://en.wikipedia.org/wiki/Ecosystem

> An **ecosystem** is a community of living organisms (plants, animals, and microbes) in conjunction with the nonliving components of their environment (things like air, water, and mineral soil) interacting as a system. These biotic and abiotic components are regarded as linked together through nutrient cycles and energy flows. As ecosystems are defined by the network of interactions among organisms and between organisms and their environment, they can be of any size but usually encompass specific, limited spaces (although some scientists say that the entire planet is an ecosystem).

Natural ecosystems include reefs, rainforests, organic farms, and even our entire planet or universe. Man-made ecosystems would include communities, cities, and networks.

Seeing the Bigger Interconnected Picture...

Let me share a few more examples I've helped conceive.

I had one gentleman come to me in the corporate training market. They had certain relationships already with companies for certain types of training areas. I had him create a powerful triad ecosystem model that brought together content experts, people that wanted to do the actual training (trained by the content expert), and companies buying the training for their employees.

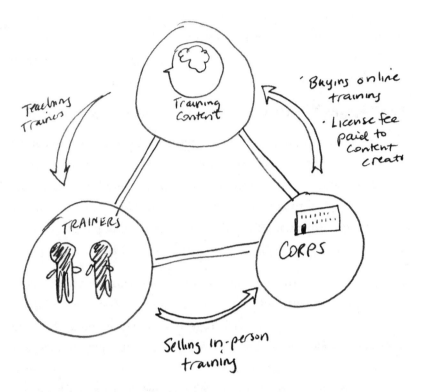

Triangulation Impact

Circling back to Bruce Poon Tip from G Adventures, he has a triangular theory of how a non-profit can work with a for-profit company. They created the **Planeterra** non-profit that also works with other companies but is funded by their travel adventures. The non-profit controls and regulates the projects done in the areas where G Adventures runs trips. The for-profit company would make it a financial success, and the local community (the third part of the triangle) works with both groups. This actually builds a sustainable advantage and delivers a more meaningful experience for their travelers.

One of the first starts was in the jungles of Bolivia. They brought in locals, many of whom had been at war with each other for generations, to see if they could build an eco-lodge. Working with an NGO partner and providing the initial capital, G Adventures then sent their tours through that area to make a stop at the Chalalan lodge. This creates a win for everyone, and they decided to start their own separate foundation, Planeterra, to do these triangulation projects more quickly.

Ecosystem That Grows Everyone in the Network

To give you a glimpse at my latest thinking, I want to show you an Evolved Enterprise to support orphans in Haiti. For the past five years, Maverick members have raised over $500,000 to build self-sustaining villages in Haiti through **Caring House Foundation** (Frank-mckinney. com/caring_project.aspx). And our on-the-ground partner is **Hope2Haiti** (HopetoHaiti.com), which is run by Scott Bonnell.

On a recent trip, a group of Mavericks and guests made a commitment to create a for-profit, self-sustaining business to fund Hope2Haiti's work with orphanages in Haiti. Together we developed an Evolved Enterprise model that helps in so many different ways and uses ecosystem thinking. It started with some sleuthing about what kinds of things have sold before to donors. When Scott mentioned Christmas greeting cards, I thought we were onto something. And I knew there was something big when he also mentioned their **"10 for Them"** program that for just $10/month can support an orphan living with a foster family.

Boom!

We brought both together with the idea to provide beautiful, hand-drawn artwork from Haitian orphanages as thank you cards. The hook is they come 10 to a pack, and we donate "Ten for Them." That's $10.00 per month going to support one Haitian child in desperate need, providing the essentials of food, clean water, shelter, clothing, and even an education.

It works for everyone, and it's not just a handout.

The customer wins because there is real scientific evidence that gratitude increases your happiness level. And a simple handwritten note goes a long way for increased connections and relationships. (Actually, I'm continually astonished at how much impact a handwritten thank you note actually gets in this digital age. I have a blog post on the long-lost art of handwritten notes here: yaniksilver.com/handwritten-note.)

I could easily see an entrepreneur or business owner buying this for their team to send out thank you notes on a regular basis. And that's another key point: This subscription pack appears each month and practically forces the recipient to use them with the people that matter most in their lives.

On the ground in Haiti, there are immense benefits. This venture would help pay the established artists who are providing art instruction to the orphans. Haitian artists are some of the best in the world, and this type of creative outlet is proven to help bolster people's happiness. And one of the orphans each month would receive a scholarship for creating the artwork selected for the monthly design.

We've just pulled together a beta test with a young entrepreneur driving this project. Check out **10CardsofHope.com** for details.

As you can see, there are so many interconnected pieces beyond just a donation. It's a massive value-add on each side. As the subscriber, I'm not just buying these thank you cards because they help someone but because they help me too. That's a key distinction. There has to be a marketplace-driven value for everyone. An Evolved Enterprise is not about guilt-driven marketing and solicitations but actually being a greater benefit and value for everybody involved.

Ecosystem thinking is absolutely in place for a potential project that's just starting to emerge, called the **Purpose Hotel** (thePurposeHotel. com), the brainchild of celebrity photographer Jeremy Cowart, who envisions a 1-for-100 benefit model each time you stay here. Jeremy launched this idea as a crowdfunding campaign on Kickstarter and got great traction but wasn't able to meet his original $2 million goal. So he reduced his budget and the project scope to a smaller $347,000 goal. Jeremy shattered this by raising $679,587 from over 4,200 backers.

Crowdfunding on Kickstarter or IndieGoGo is an excellent way to actually test out an idea before you fully commit because you can see if there is a market of buyers willing to pay for your product or service. I'm a big believer in allowing potential customers to vote with their wallets, not their opinions or surveys.

The Purpose Hotel concept is exciting because of how many interconnected pieces of impact there are entwined with your stay. The way Jeremy envisions the guest experience is something like this:

> *"When you arrive and check in, you automatically become a member of the community. Your receipt and online account show your individual impact and the collective influence of people choosing The Purpose Hotel. It adds up quickly. Under the room number outside your door, you see a boy or girl who your room helps gives access to education, food, clothing and more. Inside your room, you relax in a plush, modern place where you can learn about every object in the room and why it was selected."*

It's exciting to see these kinds of projects get traction and organically gather momentum.

The Platform Wins

Thomas Edison "won" by creating an entire ecosystem for his invention of electricity. He created the bulbs, the power stations, and the wiring, among other pieces of the platform. Everything works together, and the entrepreneur that can co-create the platform or interconnected ecosystem is the one that can have the biggest impact.

Built-in Ways Evolved Enterprises Can Create an Impact

Your business actually has significant leverage that might be under-used or underappreciated. No matter the size or scope of your company, you already have different ways you can consider applying the Evolved Enterprise concepts without really spending an extra dollar.

1. **Distribution channels.** Think about what your "voice" can do via your email list, social followings, database, package inserts, etc.

2. **Skills.** Harness the specialized talents of your team, and put them to work to help causes that resonate with you. You can even micro-volunteer online.

3. **Your product or services offered.** Through the offerings you put out, you can make a difference.

4. **Ideas.** Use your entrepreneurial brainpower to make a difference for organizations that matter.

5. **Employment/supply chain.** Who you buy from can be a significant source of redirecting your already existing expenditures or perhaps going further with the model of Empowered Employment.

What did I miss? Any other Evolved Enterprise Impact Models you've seen that might not fit these categories? Great examples you want to share or talk about?

Join the conversation to discuss and connect on these ideas in the private Facebook community for Evolved Entrepreneurs:

www.EvolvedEnterprise.com/resources

CHAPTER FOUR

DOORS WILL OPEN

Sometimes the Universe just sends you a message you cannot ignore. I call these little "winks," and I got a big one at this trendy LA restaurant where a group of Mavericks celebrated my 40th birthday.

Hanging on one of the walls was an actual door with the words "Doors will open. Follow your bliss." It showed up just as I'd been intensely studying material on the hero's journey we all seem to go on.

The quote on the door is a paraphrase of one of my favorite Joseph Campbell quotes:

> *"Follow your bliss and the universe will open doors where there were only walls."*

Campbell was a mythology expert and author of *Hero with 1,000 Faces*, who studied the "Hero's Journey" and how in a multitude of cultures, this hero's story is played out over and over again.

This notion of following your bliss is a bit misunderstood.

It's not just total pleasure floating from one fun thing to another. It's closer to utilizing all your talents, skills, resources, and passion to bring your full heart into your greatest work. Bliss appears with your most unique and ultimate expression of your best self. A complementary concept is Dan Sullivan's "Unique Ability." This is the process of identifying your best habits with the continual improvement, passion, and energy derived from performing that activity. (Dan Sullivan's team created an excellent new book entitled *Unique Ability 2.0: Discovery*, co-written by Catherine Nomura, Julia Waller, and Shannon Waller.)

Unique Ability® is not only about something that is a strength for you but something you love and that gives you more energy when you do it! Critical difference. You could have a strength, but you might not necessarily want to keep doing that activity.

And then the ultimate evolution is not being attached to the outcome.

Oof!...

This has been one of the biggest realizations I've added to my worldview.

In the outstanding book *The Great Work of Your Life*, author Stephen Cope covers the concept of dharma, a Buddhist concept essentially meaning your path or truth. (My copy is massively highlighted, and I couldn't recommend it more.)

This book is based on the two-thousand-year-old spiritual tome, the Bhagavad-Gita, and how it applies today. Cope provides numerous examples of exceptional individuals who found their dharma.

And one of the prime lessons here is "Let go of the fruits." The exact quote from the Gita is:

> *"You are only entitled to the action, never to its fruits. Do not let the fruits of action be your motive, but do not attach yourself to nonaction."*

In other words, give yourself entirely to your work, but let go of the attachment to the results.

Huh?

So here's the paradox. By putting your full heart and 100% effort into something, you actually win. Putting in the work (if it's from a true place of meaning) is enough reward.

It's only the attachment to results that creates disappointment, frustration, depression, etc. Think about it—when you have expectations and they aren't met, you're upset, right? And if we're waiting on outside praise or recognition, we're always beholden to it.

By simply having no attachment, you are free. Easier said than done because as entrepreneurs, we are typically so intermeshed into our business that our identities are wrapped up tight into whether it's a "success" or "failure."

Our whole self-worth sometimes seems to hinge on our balance sheet.

But the secret is to separate those two.

Again, this is a paradox since I've said before that the Evolved Enterprise comes out of our true being and essence—so can you separate that?

The separation comes from not being attached to the fruit or result but still putting your full effort in as your return. I get it—this idea of not being attached to any outcomes is not as fun for our right-brained, pragmatic side, so I was given another lesson...

How do we reconcile the notion of having goals?

It's true that whatever and wherever we bring the spotlight of our attention to will gain energy, grow, and "show up" (just like me "finding" that cool door while studying Campbell).

Goal setting creates some of the focused awareness on your intended course—but usually not in the way you might have been taught. Throughout the last 20 or so years, since I became a student of success traits, I've tried numerous experiments. I remember my first time being really exposed to goal setting was at a Brian Tracy seminar. I think I was probably 22 or so at the time, and Brian had us write out our 10 most important goals we truly wanted. I can't remember all 10, but I remember one of the goals was owning a Mercedes SLK.

Interestingly enough, I misplaced that workbook and found it a few years later. I think something like 7 out of 10 of the goals were hit, though the more interesting thing was that most were even "better" than what I originally wrote. For example, I had made more income than I wrote, and I ended up getting a much cooler Mercedes—SL55 AMG.

Seeing how that came together, I then changed up how I wrote my goals to add the words "or better," "or sooner," and "or more," thus giving myself more flexibility around what I was working toward. However, that once again shifted…

The New Way to Better Goal Setting for Evolved Entrepreneurs

Recently I really feel like I have an even better method that strikes to the heart of what I really, really, really want.

About four to five years ago I wrote out in my journal what my ideal day was like when I was to turn the big 4-0. I wrote out some specifics about net worth, the car I was driving, what I was doing that day, etc., trying to really capture my ideal, perfect day upon reaching my fourth decade. Well, a few weeks before my milestone birthday, I went back and found that entry. At first glance, I was a little taken aback because I didn't really hit that many of the specific goals.

I told Missy about the entry, and after seeing what I wrote, she asked if I was upset that it wasn't quite here. I thought about it for a second and said, "No."

And that's because the essence of the goals were there and even exceeded.

For instance, one thing I wrote down was that I was driving a blue Fisker Karma.

I wasn't. I already mentioned that I had actually sold my Aston Martin a few years back and wasn't interested in buying another exotic car. Instead of driving a specific car, I would rather figure out what the feeling behind the car I want is. To me, it's about having joy and

87

satisfaction from driving it and something that reflects a bit of my fun-loving spirit. (Interestingly enough, I would have regretted getting a Fisker with all the issues they had.)

The dollar amount I wrote in my journal was $2M in profits coming in from various business ventures per year. Nope, wasn't there either.

But what's the real essence behind that? To me, it's the freedom to work on what you want, with whom you please, and on what gets you excited!

Actually, I don't need two mil a year to have that, and you wouldn't either. I already have the essence of that goal. It's just about creating freedom from passive income or designing your business to support your most important contributions.

I had also jotted down other specific goals too, including giving away $5,000,000 to cause partners. Sometimes those goals that still match up your deep passion and purpose are coming. It's just not the right time. But like a train coming down the tracks...you know it's coming. In this instance, I didn't hit the $5M in charity contributions, but we are at $3.3M+ and even more when you factor in the ripple effect through other members. Once again, the essence is there.

Allowing Something Better

One interesting goal I had written down was that by the age of 39, I would go into space on Virgin Galactic. Well...that timing is not of my own doing. It's still happening, and I can continue to savor the anticipation.

Coincidentally, Virgin Galactic threw a party for 400+ future astronauts exactly on my 40th birthday. They hosted a big "Behind the Hangar Doors" event in Mojave right on September 25, so that's why I was even in the Los Angeles area in the first place.

Richard Branson had factored into my journal entry about my 40th. Here's what I wrote:

"In a few weeks the family is going to Necker Island again with Maverick members and Richard. It's become a yearly tradition since 2011, when they first came. I was just reminded of the trip because Richard sent over a wonderful surprise gift for my birthday."

I have been truly blessed to do an annual Maverick trip to Necker each year with Richard hosting—and it has become a family tradition. (We invite a select group of impactful entrepreneurs each year. More details at **Maverick1000.com/necker**.)

And Richard did send me over a surprise birthday gift by way of a personal video that was pretty funny. But even better, I spent time with him on my birthday for the Virgin Galactic event and again roughly a week later when I was invited to a safari in South Africa to support his foundation. Amazing!

All of this is something I couldn't have pictured happening in this way or scripted it out any better. That's why having the essence of what you want works. It gives you the flexibility of not being attached to how you think something will appear. I'm always in awe of the surprising new paths opening up or meeting the right person or being handed the right book that allows your "goals" to unfold in extraordinary and wonderful ways.

The requests most of us make are for things (better car, bigger house, closing the deal, etc.) and are not at the same level as requests that come from your heart and a deeper place.

> **"Learning to receive is learning to ask for the essence of what you want, rather than the form."**
> —Sanaya Roman

As you play with these Evolved Enterprise concepts, you'll start to develop a sense of when to push and when to just allow.

There's a dance of active action and receiving.

Doing and being.

It's that perfect point, like when pressing in a clutch on a steep hill. By exploring and experimenting, you'll find that balance of stopping your backwards momentum and shifting into gear—all without stalling.

This lesson really struck me when I was in Baja, Mexico, racing dune buggies with Maverick members. Imagine this: One of the sections had hairpin switchbacks with no guardrails about 4000+ feet above the valley floor. And to make it more interesting, I had no reverse gear in my car. The turns were so tight that I needed to bounce the car off the side of the mountain to roll it back while pressing in the clutch and then engaging it again before we tumbled off the side of the mountain. Trust me, you're pretty focused at that kind of moment and definitely in flow.

Engage Your Own Clutch

Pushing in the clutch is the only way to make the car really move forward from a standstill. Plus, to continue driving smoothly, you'll also need to push in the clutch, shifting from one gear to the next.

(Interestingly enough, as you move into the higher gears, you need less clutch—so it's a really good analogy here too.)

The things that keep us stuck in first gear are our own stories, habits, beliefs, actions, etc., and your own growth and evolution is the clutch to get you moving forward. (That's why the Evolved Enterprise framework starts there.)

But just to clarify, this isn't some super serious reprimand to not have any fun anymore. That would totally suck! The most evolved people I know are also the most fun and playful. Their magical inner child is a huge part of how they live their life. Even the Dalai Lama, who has just about every reason in the world to be serious, calls himself a "professional laugher."

With an Evolved Enterprise, there really isn't much difference between work and play. Play is the path to experiment and explore the intersection of more profits, more fun, and more impact—starting first with you.

YOU

"Know Yourself"

CHAPTER FIVE

HOW ENTREPRENEURSHIP CAN BE THE ULTIMATE EXPRESSION OF ARTISTRY AND LOVE

Yikes! We're going to talk about a four-letter word in business...
LOVE!

Running your enterprise from the fullest expression of love can and
will create the meaningful success that matters.

What does the "fullest expression of love" actually look like?

Like anything and everything, it always starts with YOU. Our responsibility is always on our shoulders first. And looking at the Evolved
Enterprise diagram, the founder (YOU) is at the center because a business is a reflection of the leader's evolutionary awakening.

Sleepwalking

Even if someone appears to be successful, they still could very well be
living in a slumbering state of half-hearted effort. Frankly, I've made
a lot of money without fully applying myself.

As entrepreneurs, if we get some of the basics right around delivering exceptional value, we can do well. I've seen it over and over again
with individuals seeming to have a great business, but they are not
fulfilled at a deeper level. They think business is just business and don't
consider how it could be their art. Then that lack of energy carries
over to your team, your work, and your customers. Truly everything.

One of my favorite questions during this seemingly dark period was
"What would you do even if you knew it would fail?"

This is inspired by Brene Brown's book, *Daring Greatly*, and it makes
you think if whatever you're doing is truly worth your life's energy or
not. It's an even better question than one you may have heard before:
"What would you do if you knew you couldn't fail?" The refined version
forces you to consider putting in your full heart and soul regardless
of the outcome.

So if you can truly awaken from the autopilot nature of where you are, you can start to stir a deeper sense of direction. And that inner guide has the key to what you can be doing to reinvent or rework your company or yourself.

And at the highest expression is LOVE.

You can love yourself and honor yourself in many ways. It takes time, and it's an ongoing process. I'll recommend my friend Kamal Ravikant's book, *Love Yourself Like Your Life Depends on It.*

It's a very personal story about the journey Kamal took as CEO of a venture-backed company in Silicon Valley and how he went from depression and blackness to fully engaged and living at an optimal level. You'll have to challenge yourself to do the exercises in the book for significant results.

When you're fully utilizing everything you were designed to do, there's a complete sense of divine inspiration, and time stands still. The more you can truly "know yourself," the better you can recognize where your sweet spot is. I've taken multiple personal assessment tests and would recommend Wealth Dynamics, Strengthfinders, Kolbe, and the Enneagram. Everything helps you get a little more insight into where you show up in your best way.

And when you can find that ideal merging of what you were "designed" to do, who you want to truly help, and the positive marketplace profit potential—you've won. I look at it like chipping away at everything that is not your greatest expression.

As the great artist Michelangelo said about his process, "Every block of stone has a *statue* inside it, and it is the task of the *sculptor* to discover it."

The best part is you are always provided feedback along the way of what works and what comes easily. When you're in flow, it's not an uphill slog. Personally, I use my energy level as a gauge to know if I'm on purpose or not.

I also believe you need to give yourself credit for the "R&D" (Research and Development) along the way.

This provides you with a bigger WHY you are the person to accomplish what you really want. My R&D list included a full page in my journal of everything from different business models, key connections, learnings, "failures," skill sets, and more. All of them count. **Look backwards, and embrace your past "failures" as "R&D."**

I firmly believe you cannot simultaneously have within you a deep, deep desire for creating something great without also possessing the capabilities, talent, and abilities to make it happen.

But to get there, you still might need to polish up a few things you've neglected along the way and dive deeper...

Aligning With Your Shadow

Part of my exploration has also been through casting light on my "shadow." This is a Jungian concept for a part that we want to repress and hold back, typically from the light. And many times it comes up in all sorts of ways. It could be road rage and yelling at other people in traffic in front of your kids; it could be sexually acting out; it could be continually beating yourself up for not being good enough. One way you can often recognize a shadow is a behavior you see in others that elicits a charged reaction in you that really bothers you.

Essentially, everyone around you can be a mirror for yourself, and if there's something that bothers you—usually it's because you have this behavior and haven't acknowledged it. Many times just bringing awareness to your shadow is a fast step forward to integrating it more fully into who you are.

Personally, one my biggest shadows was the recognition I was never giving 100%.

I could see an interesting pattern looking back on my life. For instance, in college, I'd go out the night before a big exam, come in late into the lecture hall smelling like bourbon, borrow a pencil, and be the first one out. Even with that, I'd still get a solid B. And with my businesses, I've always done well and over delivered, but I've never totally and absolutely given my EVERYTHING. Now if I'm being totally honest, it's probably because that leaves a little room to justify results if they are not what I had hoped for.

I feel like a broken record here, but—echoing *The Great Work of Your Life*—by putting your full essence behind something, you let go of the outcome because your complete effort is your reward by itself.

Loving yourself is also about taking care of yourself.

One of my very astute friends, Richard Rossi, likes to ask, "How would you treat a million-dollar racehorse? Would you feed them junk? Would you let them not get enough rest? Would they get training whenever they felt like it? Or instead, would there be consciousness and intentionality in what you do? Of course there would." And you can probably guess where Richard was going with this—you're the million-dollar racehorse. Actually, I'd bet you're worth significantly more than a mil.

But How Are You Treating Yourself?

As I began transitioning into a bigger version of myself, the same playbook I was using before just didn't seem like it fit me anymore.

And that's probably good because that's helped me grow exponentially as an entrepreneur and individual. Simply put, what you do each day has a compound effect on your life, your happiness, and your outlook.

Not surprisingly, there are certain combinations that create "good" days and others that have more depressing effects. Of course, everyone has their own version, but I wanted to see what universally works with experiments on myself.

I have a serious stack of books in my library on the subjects of happiness, philosophy, and self-development. From everything I've applied, studied, and done for the last twenty years, there are nine categories I've created as the "Divine 9":

1. Meaning
2. Movement
3. Mix
4. Master(y)
5. Mindfulness
6. Mentor/Mentee
7. Multiply
8. Momentum
9. Magic

I named this process the **Daily Return Path to Bliss, Joy, and Happiness,** and it's been part of my experiment to see how I can purposely work on making sure I'm the best I can be.

You can find out exactly how to apply the Daily Return Path to Bliss, Joy, and Happiness here:

www.EvolvedEnterprise.com/resources

As I'm writing this chapter, I can honestly say I'm in my best physical, mental, and spiritual place ever. I'm happier, more content, and more at peace. When you're on purpose and in alignment with your head, heart, and higher purpose, you want to be your optimal self.

Am I perfect? No, not at all, but I know I'm consistently evolving and growing.

Loving yourself fully changes the dynamics of how everyone around you reacts to you too. Because if you're honoring your vision, there's no time to say "Yes" when you really should be saying "No" to things that don't support this.

So many entrepreneurs I know are wired to be giving, but they don't make space for themselves, and then they don't have the bandwidth to help anyone else.

One of my most recent practices to honor myself has been meditating (#5: Mindfulness).

I decided to make a commitment to the practice when I interviewed Russell Simmons for a private Q&A and yoga session held with Maverick members. We discussed his latest book, *Success Through Stillness*, that's devoted to meditation, yoga, and a deeper stillness applied to business. I would highly recommend it. Russell's deep conviction really impressed me, so I figured I'd give it a try. I never thought I could do it, because I have so many ideas going around in my head, but you just keep at it. So far I'm at 15–20 minutes per day in the morning for nearly three years and going strong. The effects have been profound for me, but it's not an instant fix; it's a practice. I feel more grounded and tapped into knowing the next direction to take in my companies. These moments of stillness also help me gain clarity on what's important and what's not.

I have frequent conversations now with so many other entrepreneurs who meditate as it's becoming way more common in business circles. And there's good reason as there's mounting scientific evidence of meditation's positive effects.

Working on your own evolution is totally holographic for your business because everything really stems from you as the leader, meaning a single change to "you" creates a change in your business too. You've probably heard it before, but it is true that our outside world becomes a mirror for what's going on inside.

No matter where you are in your business or personal life, the best place for "working" through all of this on paper has always been in my journal.

The Power of Journaling

One of the most influential tools you can use to enhance your entrepreneurial life is a journal. And the best part is it only takes you about 15 minutes to see results. A journal might look like a bunch of blank pages bound together, but really, there's magic here!

There is proven scientific evidence on how journaling can make you happier.

You've probably heard previously about journaling but either thought it was too easy or too silly or just didn't know how to do it. Trust me, it works. I've been doing it for years and believe it's a total game changer.

Simply taking 10–15 minutes each day to journal will significantly impact your well-being. Journaling about an issue or thought has been proven to provide an increase in self-esteem and happiness.

The process of "expressive writing" helps to put a story line to what you're feeling.

When the thoughts roll around in our head, they just keep surfacing, being ignored and pushed back down, resurfacing, all jumbled together...so write about it.

Typing is not the same—paper and ink create a link that's unmatched. I believe handwriting actually connects your heart and mind together.

Another heavy use of my journal is taking note of what's going well through gratitude journaling. Write down absolutely everything you are grateful for. It might sound too easy, but once again, it's been scientifically proven to make us feel better. And I really do mean everything. Spend 5–15 minutes, and you'll come up with some good stuff. All of us seem to quickly adapt to any changes (good or bad), so focusing on what we're grateful for slows us down to appreciate it. And being grateful connects you to the source of your abundance—creating even more.

Positive Progress

For some reason, we're more easily focused on the stuff that goes wrong than on what is going well. And that leads to us just focusing on what else is wrong...and what else...and what else—creating an ever-building flurry of negative observations.

I like the question of **"What's going well right now?"** or **"What am I making positive progress on?"** and then simply writing in my journal.

Dan Sullivan talks about this with the analogy of the horizon: about how we are not upset that we can never reach the horizon if we are driving or walking—but somehow we want to reach our ideal. The ideal is a moving point just like the horizon, and that's why it's important to focus and reflect on where you've been and how much progress you've made. And this focus always builds up confidence, momentum, and positive energy.

You can also use your journal for working through ideas on paper or even describing your perfect day or business venture. There's pretty much no wrong way to journal. Some people will keep different journals just for ideas or separate projects. I typically just keep one and put everything in there, from my doodles, inspirational quotes, new ideas, and everything in between.

Use compelling questions as idea starters to get you writing.

The Power of Questions

I absolutely love questions...

I think questions dictate your answers, and the more powerful questions you ask, the better the answers are in life and business. Our minds want to search for answers.

I like writing down my question on the top of a page on my journal and then working on multiple answers. Most times the first answers you get will be pretty pedestrian and won't have much creativity to them. Keep pushing yourself to come up with more distinctions and sometimes even wilder answers. Don't censor yourself either—just write. Here are a couple questions to get you going as you engage in this process:

- **10 years from now, would I be happy with what I'm still doing?**
- **Who else has more to gain than I do from this succeeding? (Good question for finding partners)**
- **What is the essence of what I want?**
- **How can I provide 10x–100x in value for my customers/ clients/patients/members?**
- **What would XXX do in this situation? (i.e., mentor you look up to who can be alive or dead)**
- **What would I do even if I knew it would fail?**

And as I'm contemplating bigger decisions, I've borrowed a question from Brian Johnson, creator of Philosophers Notes: **What would my 111-year-old self tell me?**

Taking Journal Writing Even Further

Ready to really step this up?

My friend Bill Donius is the author of *Thought Revolution*. He presented a special workshop just for Mavericks, teaching us his creative method of problem solving. Typically, he only leads innovation and ideation sessions for big-name Fortune 500 clients. The book outlines the technique that helped him in his role as CEO of Pulaski Bank in St Louis. He led the bank through a successful IPO in 1998 and grew it eight-fold in size to $1.4 billion in assets.

This stuff is fascinating and extremely impactful.

You'll learn how to activate the neural pathways to unlock the right-hand side of your brain, the place responsible for creativity, intuition, wholeness, dreams, and problem solving too. Since 92% of us are right-handed, you will use your non-dominate hand (i.e., left hand) to activate the thinking and writing process.

And don't worry if you think writing with your alternative hand will be completely illegible—try it. There's something about it that creates a more child-like state of free flow. Start off easy. He recommends answering the question "If I were an animal, what animal would I be?" Answer with your dominant hand first and then, using his methodology, you'll have to suspend disbelief to allow an answer to flow from your right brain to your non-dominant hand. For me, I started as an "otter" (playful, etc.), but my left-handed response was "sea turtle." I think of *Finding Nemo* and the 150-year-old sea turtle with his laid-back wisdom!

He says the animal we choose with our dominant hand typically represents an aspirational choice, while the animal we choose with our non-dominant hand represents a truer version of ourselves.

The results will astound you.

By activating the right brain, I've been able to tap into answers that I never would have imagined and to have the confidence that I'm getting guidance from a more elevated self. It sounds a little weird, but there's a profound knowing that the answers carry even more weight. I'd also suggest using the previous questions you've answered with your dominant hand and exploring them with this process.

Evolving yourself is not a "one and done" kind of job, because everything here cascades down over the whole company from the inside out. It's ongoing and something that continues to pay dividends over and over again.

CAUSE

THOSE WHO HAVE A 'WHY' TO LIVE,
CAN BEAR ALMOST ANY 'HOW'
— Viktor Frankl

CHAPTER SIX

WHAT IS YOUR WHY?

Finding your WHY is the core nucleus and driver for what you're doing. If your answer is to get rich, then I'd argue that's not enough. Sure, it can be a motivator, but it's not going to sustain you through the ups and downs of business or to actually build something meaningful. And the fact is, I've never seen anybody truly succeed in the long run by only looking at what they're going to get.

In one of my first journals 15 years ago, I wrote a core value of *"I get rich by enriching others 10 times to 100 times what they pay me in return."*

That's become my internal formula to judge a project or offering by because it's in synch with an unyielding natural law. Not surprisingly, when you deliver that much value, the marketplace compensates you accordingly. This goes along with a famous quote motivational speaker Zig Ziglar frequently used: *"You can get anything you want if you help enough people get what they want."*

Taken another way, the Evolved Enterprise can serve the greatest collective good yet still remain totally self-serving for you—a beautiful notion of what actually is best for the whole is best for you.

The marketplace is always self-correcting. So the only real strategy to enduring and lasting wealth is to over-deliver as much as you can and provide just as much value.

Now you can turbo charge that with an authentic cause or big reason why you're actually in business.

I saw this first hand with my eleven-year-old dude, Zack.

For the past six years, we've put on a Family Freedom event for kids ages 6–16, tailored to their interests and comprehension. We have some fun family experiences, sessions for parents, and specific ones for the kids. Then the kids break up into teams to learn about business and run different ventures. (Maverick1000.com/family)

Several years back we held the event over July 4th, so the kids were selling related products and services. They had to create their own promotions and pricing, understand their budgets, and market them to the 4th of July crowd.

My son Zack is a little less outgoing than his younger sister, Zoe, but when we added a charitable component to his team's venture, he couldn't be stopped. They were selling glow sticks, and his opening pitch was "Save the Bay—buy a glow stick." I've never seen him so committed before, and it was because he was also helping a cause bigger than just himself. I was really proud of him.

Save the Bay was because we were in Annapolis, MD, right on the Chesapeake Bay. Linking to a cause that's central to you or your customers in an authentic way makes a dramatic difference. I have no doubt his sales increased, and they even got just straight-up donations from people without them buying a glow stick.

This is a small example, but when you truly tie in something that really fits, you see dramatic jumps.

Working with Maverick NEXT* member Anthony Balduzzi, we developed a key cause that truly made sense around his life story. Anthony was already doing well with his health and fitness information publishing business but was in the midst of a serious rebranding initiative. He had put a lot of thought into both the updated website design and revamped brand messaging to specifically niche down to helping men over 40 lose weight and regain their energy—but I didn't think that was enough.

Here's how Anthony describes our work together:

"Our big aim with the rebranding was to empower our information publishing business model to have a far greater social impact than simply selling eBooks and weight loss courses online. Within the first 10 minutes of the call, Yanik adeptly assessed the strong, unexploited niche that our rebranded

109

business could become a market leader in: helping <u>fathers over 40</u> lose weight and regain their vibrant health.

With our more focused audience in place, Yanik then helped us construct a new product offering (weight loss challenge for charity) that would help increase our revenue, improve our customer experience, and enable our brand to have the social impact we wanted with our rebrand with 10x the potential brand impact."

It all started with Anthony's story that I helped dig out to make a more meaningful connection to his cause. Tragically, Anthony's father died from brain cancer just before his 10th birthday, and that created a burning desire to help that's never gone away. Together, we came up with the concept for "Fit Father Project" (FitFatherProject.com), and it's full steam ahead for him. He says it on his site:

I promised Dad that no fathers would ever have to go through his pain and lack of health. Not on my watch. And I set out on a 10-year mission to figure out exactly how men get (and stay) healthy for life. I know it's what Dad would have wanted.

We worked on matching up this compelling story with a cause that would matter and really fit here. Going back to the time when he was a kid, he picked Camp Kesem as their cause because they put kids into summer camp whose parents are battling cancer. He has a real innovative model we developed to make a difference:

We donate a baseline 10% of all our profits to Camp Kesem. For every pound you lose on any of our programs, we donate an additional $1 directly to a Camp Kesem attendee fund.

*Maverick NEXT is an invite only network of young entrepreneurs, ages 25 and under, who already have some success in business but feel that they are destined for something much greater...in their entrepreneurial endeavors and contribution to the world. (MaverickNEXT.com)

Now, if you're paying attention, you noticed Anthony's compelling story. We'll talk more about that in the next section because it's such a huge component here. All of these elements work in concert together and synergistically create a greater whole than the sum of their parts.

The Evolved Enterprise, **Beyond Meat** (beyondmeat.com), is a huge potential success story in the making, disrupting a mega multi-billion-dollar industry of pro-  tein. Perhaps you've seen their products in Whole Foods? The burgers are actually placed next to the meat section in their stores, and the last few times I've been there, they've had a hard time keeping them in stock. I'm a huge fan of their burgers made from "plant protein" that actually sizzle and "bleed" beet juice. My wife thinks it looks and tastes almost too real. Our son, Zack, who is a huge cheeseburger connoisseur, has actually been swayed to go part-time to these better-for-you burgers.

The founder and CEO of Beyond Meat, Ethan Brown, believes there is a better way to feed the planet. Their mission is to create mass-market solutions that perfectly replace animal protein with plant protein. In the process, that improves human health, positively impacting climate change, conserving natural resources, and respecting animal welfare. And in a recent interview in *Conscious Company* magazine, he provided the advice "Make sure the business's mission is what you want to accomplish in your life…If you feel you're truly on a mission in your heart and your spirit, you can tap into something that's much greater than just building a successful business for monetary reasons."

Another company with a noble mission around food is **Two Degrees Foods** (TwoDegreesFoods.com), and they clearly state their reason why on their site:

> ## We fight childhood hunger. It's why we exist.
> ### We do this by asking people to reconsider their daily purchases.
>
> *At 2 Degrees Food, we believe that your everyday purchase choices have a big impact. Instead of grabbing just any snack, you can now choose one that feeds your hunger and helps do the same for a hungry child. **That's the power of the Buy-One-Give-One model: For every 2 Degrees bar you buy, we feed a hungry child.***

They're using the 1-for-1 model to create a direct impact to feed one child when you purchase a bar. To date, they've donated over 1,000,000 meals by working with several on-the-ground cause partners in different areas of the world.

I first heard of Two Degrees food bars on a United flight because they were one of the featured in-air snacks for purchase. And that's another HUGE bonus you'll see when you apply the Evolved Enterprise concepts in a genuine way—bigger companies will look to potentially partner with you. If you choose the bigger partner correctly, it's a good move for everybody. You get to benefit from their increased distribution and exposure, and they get a bit of your halo effect. And not only will partners be interested but the press will be intrigued too if you are making a genuine difference.

Inauthentic Hurts More Than It Helps

Picking your cause should have either personal significance for you or be tied back to your product in an area that your customers would want to see their support go to. If you are just trying to piggyback on a cause to get "brownie points," you might get some bump in sales and revenue, but you won't see a dramatic lift in team engagement or customers actually becoming serious advocates for you. You see this with multi-nationals that simply add a charity component without really considering how it fits into their overall DNA more deeply.

In a 2010 KFC campaign, they put out pink buckets of chicken to fight breast cancer. For each pink bucket of chicken, KFC would donate 50 cents to the Susan G. Komen Foundation. I didn't even see any tie-in until a friend pointed out it might be around the breasts of chickens and women. This triggered a PR disaster because one of the risk factors for breast cancer is a high-fat diet and obesity.

With the total interconnectedness of the Web, this goof creates a serious black eye for the company involved and the cause partner. That's why I believe you need to seriously consider who you partner with and in what capacity.

Choosing a Cause Partner

Some brands and businesses lend themselves more easily to work with cause partners; for instance, a food company might align with serving meals to the homeless or a food kitchen. It makes sense, and there's a perfect tie-in. However, you don't have to only be pigeon-holed based on your category. It's critical to consider your own story, what authentically fits, and also what your customers are ultimately looking for.

For example, another Maverick NEXTer I worked with was putting together a line of clothing in a very particular marketplace. (I'll keep the details a little vague since I don't want to give everything away as he is still in the process of implementing these ideas.) Now, the marketplace has some already well-defined community values in place, and we chose well-known cause partners to match the community values. We also spent a lot of time talking about identity and community (we'll cover that shortly). After the session, here's what he reported:

"I felt like applying Evolved Enterprise to our business takes it a step up, from being a basic transactional retailer, to the next level of being an entity bigger than just itself, with more purpose. Evolved Enterprise is a different type of thinking that helps focus on delivering value."

This type of thinking does take your business to another level beyond a one-dimensional, transactional company.

Another consideration could be your ingredients or components of the product. One Evolved Enterprise in Colorado is an artisan tea company, Teakoe teas. They've made commitments to build beehives based on their sales because of the importance bees have in our world. Honey is part of their iced teas, so they are using their impact here. And they have a little fun with it by saying they've impacted 20,000 jobs, talking about the bees and the number of hives they've been able to adopt. (teakoe.com/pages/thrive)

When looking for cause partners, check out **Guidestar.org** and **CharityNavigator.org**. Both of these resources will allow you to search by categories and give you a good look at the charities' ratios of serving vs. administration costs.

Choosing Between Known and Unknown Causes

One consideration is whether you partner with a well-known charity or a smaller one. With a known partner, you are getting built-in name recognition that might have a bump for you in overall sales. But with a relatively unknown partner, you are making a more direct difference. One tip: If you are going to work with a bigger cause partner and you are a smaller company, there are lots of hoops to jump through. I would make contact with a local office since they are usually much easier to work with and you get the same name recognition.

That's exactly what I did back in 2003 for my 30th birthday bash in Orlando. We held a birthday "party" for 530+ of our best customers, and the only way to get in was a $50 donation to Make-A-Wish. I worked with the Orlando chapter, and they were super excited to come in for a $25,000 check. We won because the attendees felt good about their registration fee.

Today we solely focus on entrepreneurship for our impact.

Why? Entrepreneurs are our world's catalysts. Individually, we drive growth, value-creation, and innovation. And collectively, I believe 21st-century entrepreneurs have the greatest leverage available to impact the globe.

Our Reason Why: Changing the Way Business Is Played!

Connecting and Catalyzing the World's Most Impactful Entrepreneurs, Mavericks, and Influencers to Co-Create a Meaningful Global Shift in Business

Like us, you don't have to just pick one cause partner if you don't want to. You can have certain products related to different causes that match up, like we looked at in Evolved Enterprise Impact Model #4b: Donate Where You Want.

For instance, with our Maverick Impact fund, we have helped support programs ranging from microenterprise in East Africa to ex-offenders in East LA receiving business training. To me, the theme is always around entrepreneurship and making a difference for underserved communities. Even more than cash, I'm always interested in how our Maverick network can contribute their brainpower, resources, and network to make a difference. We incorporate this in a significant way directly into each of our events and experiences, so it's not just an "oh by the way" but actually baked right in. (We'll cover this in more detail shortly in the next section too.)

As you're considering the Cause, you'll need to decide if it's simply a one-time promotional-type thing or truly built into your business in some way. No question, being truly integrated gives you a greater impact, but dipping your toes into the water with a specific cause and specific promotion is okay too. That way you can see if there really is something to the Evolved Enterprise stuff.

One more consideration is how you can leverage a cause partner in a mutually beneficial way. Make-A-Wish is probably not going to promote you to their donors, but a smaller cause might. Get creative. I know one Maverick1000 member piggybacking with some of the biggest charities because he offers them a way to tell their story better, and his material becomes a ride-along. So a nice win–win.

CREATION

DON'T resort to imitation BUT rather look for INSPIRATION to further your own CREATION

IN PURSUIT of INNOVATION

— Anonymous

CHAPTER SEVEN

BEING
EXCEPTIONALLY
DIFFERENT

Going through the Evolved Enterprise thinking process for your company will automatically make you different—but it's still up to you to make sure your customers know what you're doing differently.

One of my favorite questions I ask myself when creating new innovative offerings is **"How can I go the opposite direction of most of my competitors?"**

It's a bit like the "best of times" and the "worst of times" out there because simple online tools have made it easy for so many people to put something up in almost every single marketplace and category. Our job is to make sure that we can break through the clutter and have a unique angle, hook, and story to share with our potential customers.

There's a smart book by a Harvard professor, Youngme Moon, simply called *Different*. In the book, she talks about how companies are always looking at their competitors and trying to pick off what they're good at. They take those pieces and basically create an entire array of features and benefits that are only all sort of above average. But none of them really stand out to the customers, so there's no real differentiation point.

A really good example of going the opposite direction is our Underground® Online Seminar. It started in 2004 and had been sold out every year until we retired it after a decade. When I first started it, there were a lot of Internet marketing and online entrepreneurial events out there, but they were all roughly the same. They had the same speakers and the same sort of topics. I don't really like to do the same thing as everyone else, because there's not a real point to it.

That's when one of my buddies and I were having a drink at a hotel bar, and he was lamenting to me the fact that he just went to the seminar and it was a big "pitch fest." There was not that much content shared, and he said, "You know, what I'd like to see is a bunch of real-world people actually showing what they're doing and how they're making their money. Not ones that have made their money selling how to make money on the Internet. And you're the guy to do it—you know so many different people from different places."

I realized, *Yeah, I could probably do that.*

That's how the Underground® event was born—entirely based on the idea that there are real-world people who are out there making money who aren't selling how to make money information. And they are doing it in all different ways, shapes, and forms.

Now, I'm a big fan of creating not just a great educational experience but also creating a fun environment. At the Underground®, we made it a lot more interesting for attendees because it wasn't just a normal boring seminar. There always was a spy theme attached to it. Some years we've had celebrities like "Mini-Me" Verne Troyer, or we've brought in one of the actors who played James Bond and a star of *24*. There is usually a different theme each year. And it didn't stop there, because there are tons of great parties and experiences to make attendees bond together.

Doing things differently sometimes has a downside too. After retiring the Underground® it would have been tough to just go back with another seminar inside a hotel ballroom. That's why our team decided to innovate again and create a new annual event called Camp Maverick. It's an invitation-only summer camp for entrepreneurs to connect in truly unique ways. (**GoCampMaverick.com**)

Start with a Blank Page

Another good example is Virgin America, one of my favorite airlines. They do a lot of things right. If you look at the other airlines out there, they are all pretty much the same (even in first class). But with Virgin America, they actually started with a clean slate of paper and said, *"What isn't good about the flying experience in the USA?"* Of course, the answer is almost everything. So they went through and created a much better experience.

For instance, they added a simple but truly remarkable feature when first introduced: a power outlet in between the seats so you can keep your laptop fired up for a cross-country flight from DC to LA. They make the interior of the plane look really, really cool, with lighting that changes colors based on the time of day. Plus, they have these really white seats. When you walk onto the plane, it just looks cool and feels like a lounge. And they were one of the first to have Wi-Fi in the air. (Other airlines have since copied some of these innovations, but that's not the point.)

People are excited to fly because Virgin America's crew members also have a great attitude. A lot of this experience comes from the founder, Sir Richard Branson, and you can just see his DNA is infused into all the Virgin companies—the idea of "just a little bit cheeky" and "just a little bit fun" and "just a bit adventurous" throughout.

Create Compelling Stories

It's easier than ever to (over)share via social media, but why would a customer actually tell someone else they bought something from you?

For your message to get broadcast, it's crucial for consumers to be able to "get it" quickly and be able to connect. Over 80 years ago, one man had the answer to increasing almost any product's sales and literally crushing the competition.

His name?

Claude Hopkins. And today his advice is even more valuable than it was during the 1920s. Hopkins was one of the most famous admen and really the father of modern advertising. His two books, *My Life in Advertising* and *Scientific Advertising*, are worth reading and re-reading.

I'll share with you one of Hopkins' greatest secrets for attracting more business. Listen closely—the secret is <u>EDUCATION</u>.

By educating a prospect about how things are done in your business, even if it's the same exact thing any one of your competitors could tell, it will produce a tremendous selling advantage.

Hopkins used this advertising secret to rocket a so-so beer brand from fifth place into a tie for first place in just a matter of months. Listen to this:

Schlitz Beer hired Hopkins to increase their falling market share. At this time, every beer manufacturer was screaming "PURE" in their ads. In fact, companies were spending a fortune just advertising this four-letter word as big and as bold as they could. They even took out double-page ads to put that word in even bigger letters. All this shouting and no explaining was making zero impression on the buying public. Nobody ever explained what "pure" really meant until Hopkins came in.

The first thing Hopkins did was take a factory tour. On this tour, he was shown plate-glass rooms where beer was dripping over pipes. Inquiring about the reason for this, Hopkins was told that those rooms were filled with filtered air so the beer could be cooled without any impurities.

Next he was shown huge, expensive filters filled with white-wood pulp that provided a superior filtering process. The manufacturer then went on to explain how they cleaned every pump and pipe twice daily to ensure purity and also how each bottle was sterilized not once or twice but four times before being filled with beer.

Then Hopkins was shown the 4,000-foot-deep artesian wells dug to provide the cleanest and purest water available, even though the factory was right on the shore of Lake Michigan.

Finally, Hopkins was led into a laboratory and was shown the mother yeast cell that was a product of 1,200 experiments to bring out the robust flavor. And he was told all the yeast used in making Schlitz beer was developed from that original yeast cell.

After his tour, Hopkins exclaimed, "Why don't you tell people these things?"

The manufacturer's response was because every beer manufacturer does it the same way.

And to that, Hopkins replied, "But others have never told this story..." And he went off to create an advertising campaign explaining to people what makes Schlitz beer pure. Once again he told the same story any brewer could have, but he gave a meaning to purity. And this is what took Schlitz from fifth place to a tie for first place in market share.

Really, this whole process is just educating.

Educating prospects about the hows, the whys, the good, the bad, and the ugly. You simply cannot overeducate people.

And you have an even better secret weapon to spread your story—the impact you are making. But, and this is a key but, you have to explain it and share it in a way customers can connect with and then spread the message potentially. One of the reasons TOMS has done so well is their story is easy to understand and share. And they continue sharing the message everywhere, even on the insoles of their shoes.

If your customers are not informed and educated about why you only use sustainable fabrics, soy ink, or a certain material or how you are making a direct impact, etc.—it's as if it didn't happen. You don't get credit for it, and it doesn't become a marketing multiplier for you. You have to share your authentic impact everywhere. It can be your Impact Scoreboard on your website, your blog can be filled with stories of the difference you're making, it can be on your package insert, etc.—everything should continue educating your buyers so they can become advocates.

Look at the engaging way **Indosole** (indosole.com) uses an illustration to educate consumers on their process of recycling old tires and turning them into soles of shoes.

Must-Tell Stories

A few years ago, I was dining at Danny Meyer's Modern Restaurant in New York City with a colleague. We both ordered up the tasting course menus with all the multiple courses and a different wine with each. You know the drill.

Danny has great book out called *Setting the Table*, and he has a concept in it called "enlightened hospitality." The idea behind this is that the server should be paying enough attention to the customers that they can almost predict what's going on and help them deal with almost any unmet needs or needs that they don't necessarily verbalize.

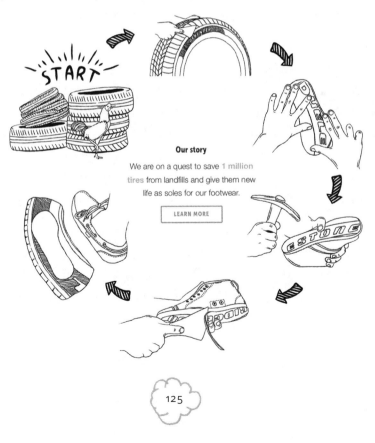

Our story

We are on a quest to save 1 million tires from landfills and give them new life as soles for our footwear.

LEARN MORE

So my dining partner and I were right behind another table where a couple was having a knock-down, drag-out sort of argument about their family. The man was complaining about his mother-in-law and holidays and how much he hated her. I can compartmentalize pretty well, so I wasn't affected, but the guy with me was getting bothered. Since the waiters were paying attention to this, they actually did something I've never seen happen before. A waiter literally came over and poured a small pitcher of water on our table and said, "Oh my God, I'm so clumsy. I can't believe I did that. I'll have to get you guys re-seated right away!" Then the staff instantly whisked away eight plates and eight wine glasses and moved us to a corner where it was a lot quieter.

Think about that. Instead of telling the other table, "Can you guys just shut the hell up?" they let the other table still "enjoy" their evening without embarrassing them and helped us enjoy our evening. This was such an exceptional experience that I've been compelled to share this story over and over again on stages and now in this book.

Another tale that's now become somewhat well known is from Tony at Zappos again. He shared the story at Underground® of a woman who bought a pair of boots for her husband. Unfortunately, her husband never got them because he was killed in a car accident. When the customer called to return the boots to Zappos and explained what happened, the rep took it upon herself to send flowers to the funeral. This created a huge stir and word-of-mouth sensation at the funeral because what online e-tailer would send flowers to someone even after they returned the product?

The big lesson here is to provide anyone who works with you enough authority and latitude to make something good happen. Allow them to deliver surprise and delight that turns regular customers into raving fans.

 **CHAPTER EIGHT**

BAKED-IN GOOD

Creating an impact is so much easier when it's just a simple habit like brushing your teeth. That's why one of the ways that works so well is for each product sold to have a direct impact provided. Many of the Evolved Enterprise Impact models we looked at earlier had an automatic impact baked right in.

Look back at a few of the highlighted companies, like Sevenly.org, which puts 7% from every order into the selected cause partner they are supporting that week. Or FEED bag serving hungry children with each bag purchase—and so many others. All of this leads to customers wanting to share their purchase and proclaim their identities tied to your product or service.

Full 360-Degree Impact

As you're examining and adding Evolved Enterprise concepts, make sure you look at each and every piece of the customer experience so it is congruent with what you espouse. One good company that gets this is **PACT** (wearpact.com). They started off a few years ago with underwear and have expanded to other categories. Here's their story (notice the creation story):

PACT is obsessed with a big idea: super soft organic cotton that makes the world a better place. Socks with soul, altruistic underwear and other everyday essentials ethically manufactured with fabrics that feel good and go easy on the environment. Sounds good? Oh it is. In fact, co-founder Jeff Denby created PACT to turn bad into good. After spending years working in the international manufacturing business with its questionable working conditions and environmental policies, Jeff decided it was time for a change. And change starts with your underwear. So at PACT our manufacturing process is designed to be good from seed to shelf. We care about our clothes so much we pretty much follow them wherever they go so customers can not only feel good in PACT but also feel good about where PACT came from. PACT is good design for good people.

I own a few pairs of PACT underwear, but what I really appreciated about them is that their packaging is in total alignment with their social good. You have to think about your "DNA" all the way through your product or service. They are a mail-order underwear company, so using the wrong packaging would absolutely be the wrong message. Here's what they say on their outside mailing envelope:

Not only do we recommend a daily change of underwear, we also recommend making a daily change in our world. This 100% compostable package is here to help with both. Just like you toss your underwear in your dirty clothes, you can literally toss this bag in with your dirt. Even the mailing label and adhesive will decompose in less than 45 days.

Now, that is in total alignment with their company values. What's more, they also do a significant job on educating consumers about the process of how the clothing is made:

Many people don't think about how their clothes are made. But, just as food doesn't come from a grocery store, clothes don't come from a department store. In fact, your clothing and food often start out in the same place: a farmer's field. PACT goes to great lengths to make sure our entire supply chain, from the growing and harvesting of the organic cotton to the final sewing and all the processes in between, are as clean and responsible as possible. We are pretty proud of how we make our stuff so you can not only feel good in your PACT clothes but feel good about where they came from too.

Marketing Through the Heart

One of the key concepts I hope you really grasp is being an Evolved Enterprise doesn't mean you aren't actively promoting.

Your gut knows if you're fudging the line a bit or not. If you wouldn't feel completely proud to put out your product/service or the marketing behind it—there's something that isn't in alignment. You have the best internal compass in the world if you actually listen. Are you completely sold on what you're doing? If not, it's time to figure out what else you can do to create a tremendous value that you would be remiss not to promote.

With an Evolved Enterprise, you can truly capitalize on your impact in significantly more ways than your "ordinary" competitors.

Originally, I wasn't going to include a few of these examples because it could easily be construed as simply a marketing tactic. But I have faith you'll apply these additional examples for a greater good or, as Newman's Own would proudly proclaim, "The shameless exploitation for the common good."

Yes, it's a bit (or a lot) tongue in cheek, but that's okay.

One of the pioneering advertising icons of the 20th century, David Ogilvy, provided this sage advice: "The consumer isn't a moron; she is your wife."

Today's consumer is armed with more information, online reviews, and insider knowledge than ever before. Think of how you want to invite people to join you instead of just selling to them using well-worn marketing tricks and tactics that just don't cut it anymore. That's actually a good thing because there's another separation between Evolved Enterprises and the rest of the pack.

Now please don't get so anti-marketing here that you throw everything out the window.

The fundamental rules for marketing will apply and will not change. You'll need to define your audience, figure out how you're going to reach them, create your compelling offer, and then provide a reason why they should act now. But you get to put your own mark on this with a totally authentic voice.

People want to buy from real people.

They want to know your story, why you're so passionate about what you're doing, and how your product or service will make a greater difference to them (and to the world).

And even better, as you build out all the different facets of an Evolved Enterprise, you actually have more opportunities to multiply your marketing efforts. Take a look at these smart marketing examples of creating compelling alignment and momentum around the impact delivered...

You have to put your full heart into products and services—but ALSO your full effort into ethically "inviting" the right prospects to buy.

The good news is you're working with a stacked deck in your favor because by combining smart marketing and promotion with an Evolved Enterprise, you get a significant boost.

What's more, you can market in ways that will make competitors shake their heads and wonder what the hell you're up to.

Reverse Pitch

I remember a Patagonia promotion that blatantly stated, "Don't Buy This Jacket."

It was Cyber Monday in 2011, and Patagonia went the opposite direction (remember that?) and said to not buy their jacket. Here's the beginning of the ad:

Today is Cyber Monday. It will likely be the biggest online shopping day ever. Cyber Monday was created by the National Retail Federation in 2005 to focus media and public attention on online shopping. But Cyber Monday, and the culture of

consumption it reflects, puts the economy of natural systems that support all life firmly in the red. We're now using the resources of one-and-a-half planets on our one and only planet. Because Patagonia wants to be in business for a good long time—and leave a world inhabitable for our kids—we want to do the opposite of every other business today. We ask you to buy less and to reflect before you spend a dime on this jacket or anything else.

This might be a bit of reverse psychology since sales were up 40% for a two-year period following this ad. I doubt it's just attributed to this campaign, but I think it's a long-term mindset about the purpose of business that's espoused by Rose Marcario, the CEO of Patagonia, here: *"Business can be the most powerful agent for change, and if business doesn't change, then I think we're all doomed. Business that puts profit above people and the environment is not going to be a healthy and sustainable way for us to live and for the planet to survive."*

This reminds me a little bit of one of the top copywriters in the 1900s, John E. Powers, who wrote this ad for a Pittsburgh department store in severe financial trouble:

"We are bankrupt. We owe $125,000 more than we can pay, and this announcement will bring our creditors down on our necks. But if you come and *buy* tomorrow, we shall have the money to meet them. If not, we shall go to the wall."

Instead of yelling "SALE" like so many other stores would, there's a legitimate reason given why people should spend their money at this store. And this ad was said to be responsible for saving the store.

Another ad written by Powers, for a different merchant, proclaimed, *"We have a lot of rotten raincoats we want to get rid of."* This sold out the entire inventory of raincoats by the next morning.

Personalize the Connection Story

Yellow Leaf Hammocks (yellow-leafhammocks.com) is working on breaking the cycle of extreme poverty through sustainable job creation. They provide weaver communities the opportunity to hand weave their hammocks and earn a healthy income. Each hammock comes with a handwritten tag that tells you the name of the person responsible for making it. This directly connects you to an individual instead of just another nameless corporation. On the site, you can read stories of the artisan weavers; like clicking on Yalana's picture, I learned this:

Yalana keeps Mlabri traditions alive with her love of music and beautiful singing voice—and her mischievous jokes! Yalana returns to the forest sometimes to reconnect with her roots, but she embraces the security and flexibility of the weaver's lifestyle. Yalana is proud to ensure that all six of her children can attend school.

Once you have that actual person-to-person human connection, you are more invested in any product or service.

Even Your Name Is Powerful

On my most recent visit to Necker Island, I noticed these new snack bars they put out for breakfast. In big, bold print, the packaging proudly proclaims, **THIS BAR SAVES LIVES**. Perfect. The name says it all.

I think one of the most overlooked aspects in your marketing is naming a product or service. There's a lot to be said of coming up with the right name that helps move the needle.

Ever heard of a Patagonian Tooth Fish? Sounds delicious, right? Not quite...but when the name was changed to "Chilean Sea Bass," sales grew dramatically. Or how about the "Chinese Gooseberry"—wouldn't you like to have that for a snack? No? Oh, okay, then maybe "Kiwi Fruit" is a better name.

Names are quite powerful, and that's just another piece to think about as you re-invent your business.

Compelling Partners

Just like the Two Degree bars with United as a partner, having a direct impact creates unique partnerships and new highly leveraged distribution opportunities. This Bar Saves Lives works with Save the Children as their cause partner to deliver packets of food to a child in need for each bar bought. Not only is the bar now getting some big-time exposure to the guests on Sir Richard Branson's private island but they also have an all-star team of business and celebrity advisors behind them. I asked the manager at Necker about the bars, and they said they bought them specifically because of the impact piece.

There's no doubt celebrities sell products and services. And as an Evolved Enterprise, you have a greater chance of getting a famous partner if you have a significant impact footprint.

A couple of years ago, for the first time, Oprah Winfrey lent her name to a brand in the name of charity. If you've been to a Starbucks or Starbucks-owned **Teavana** store, you've probably seen Oprah's Chai Tea. This is a unique power collaboration coming together under the umbrella of making a difference. Proceeds from the sale will benefit her Oprah Winfrey Leadership Academy Foundation, which supports a variety of youth education charities, from Oprah Winfrey Leadership Academy for Girls to the U.S. Dream Academy.

A business grows by getting more customers, increasing the transaction value spent, or getting more repeat customers. Your impact can actually be tied back to innovative ways of making a difference and bringing customers back in.

For the past few years Starbucks has also provided a free cup of coffee on Earth Day to anyone coming in with a reusable mug. This creates a good reason to return to Starbucks and links them to a bigger global cause.

Madewell also lets their customers recycle their jeans, but they've taken it up a notch by partnering with Blue Jeans Go Green, which turns old jeans into housing-insulation for communities in need. When a customer brings in a pair of jeans, they feel great about it and receive a $20 credit toward a new pair.

RECYCLE YOUR OLD JEANS WITH US

Did you know it takes approximately 500 to 1,000 pairs
of jeans to insulate just one home? Translation: We could really use yours.
Bring them into any of our stores, any day, year-round.
We're turning them into housing insulation for communities in need.
Read on for details.

HOW TO HELP OUT? IT'S AS EASY AS I, 2, 3.

STEP I	STEP 2	STEP 3
Bring your old (read: bottom-of-the-stack, back-of-the-closet) jeans to your local store.	We'll send them to our friends at Blue Jeans Go Green℠ to recycle into housing insulation.	You'll get $20 off a new pair of jeans—our way of saying thanks for participating.*

Last year fashion retailer **H&M** and **DoSomething.org**, one of the largest organizations for young people and social change, teamed up to get young people recycling clothing. In a campaign called "Comeback Clothes," they encouraged young people to give their old and worn-out clothing a new life through recycling. The program included a social media component with anyone taking a picture of themselves dropping off the clothes being entered to win a $10,000 scholarship and receiving a 15% discount off their next purchase.

I would imagine more than a few of the young people recycling their clothes also added a new outfit or two to their wardrobe, just like the free coffee recipients at Starbucks bought something else to eat there too.

Uncover New Distribution Channels

Pay attention because in the next chapter, we'll go deep into building communities of brand advocates and zealots. An interesting marketing application for this kind of tribe is creating ambassadors to promote for you.

Apparel company **Serengetee** does a remarkable job of using college and high school "ambassadors" to sell their product line of pocket t-shirts, tanks, backpacks, and hats. The "hook" here is that the company uses a different type of fabric from another country on each of the pockets (serengetee.com). That's the way this company has grown and carved a different niche for themselves in a crowded t-shirt space.

They're using Impact Model 4b: Donate Where You Want, with each of the different fabrics matched up against a contribution to a particular cause or charity. Serengetee has taken a really smart marketing approach in rewarding their college and high school ambassadors for being influencers on social media and authentically sharing the brand with their family and friends. The results are pretty sizeable; in the first year, they had 20,000 Facebook fans and then massively multiplied to 125,000 by year two.

Improving Shopping Cart Abandons and Generating Impact

My two friends, Josh Bezoni and Joel Marion, have grown **BioTrust Nutrition** by being committed to helping millions of people worldwide live healthier lives. And part of that commitment is making giving one of the company's core values.

Since its inception in 2012, BioTrust Nutrition has been a supporter of Make-A-Wish, and they've developed an easy way to make a difference and increase their sales. At checkout, their customers have the opportunity to donate $1, $5, or $10 at checkout when they place an order. BioTrust Nutrition will match the amount given, and they've now donated over $1 million to Make-A-Wish, helping grant more than 125 wishes for children with life-threatening medical conditions. (Notice this uses Evolved Enterprise Impact Model 4a: Donate What You Want.)

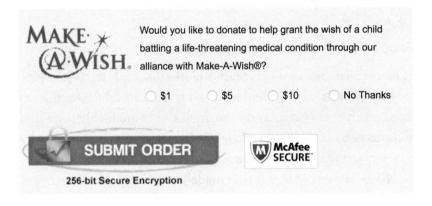

Josh and Joel are really extremely sharp at marketing and have big hearts. They've tested all sorts of ways to optimize their shopping cart and order process. And they reported to me a 15% increase in sales by A/B testing the shopping cart page with or without this giving opportunity. That's a huge stat. Any eCommerce entrepreneur will tell you their shopping cart abandons are one of the biggest areas they consistently work on to improve, and this impact addition could be a key secret.

List Building and Impact Making

Ecommerce company **Uncommon Goods** has a unique way they combine impact with their marketing too. After your purchase, you are given a choice of several non-profits to donate $1 from your order to. Then you can double the donation they will make to $2 if you spread the word via Facebook or Twitter. Smart. It works because according to the site, they've already made over $1,000,000 in contributions from their "Better to Give" program started in 2001.

This is a perfect example of considering how and where to incorporate an impact into the natural flow of your customers' interactions.

BETTER to GIVE

Thank you for selecting **ROR** to receive our $1 donation.
Spread the word, double your impact: share Better to Give with friends and we'll donate another $1 to **ROR**.

SHARE »

Proof You're Walking Your Talk

As more and more consumers see businesses that trade on their impact, they are going to want to know HOW you are making a difference. Teaming up with cause partners on the ground that are highly respected and effective is a significant advantage. This way you can show exactly how you are making a difference and where part of the consumers' purchases is going (if that is your model) with the Impact Scoreboard.

The bottom line here is to simply let your heart be your guide for the direction of your marketing and sales promotions. Become curious and open. Be on the lookout for how companies outside your industry or marketplace are doing things. See what compels you to buy, and consider if there's something there you want to bring back to your own business.

COMMUNITY

CHAPTER NINE

COMMUNITY CODE 2.0:
CREATING TRIBES OF BELOVED BRAND BUILDERS

Let's face it—companies that can harness the power of extremely loyal customers win!

They get to spend less on marketing and advertising. Their customers keep buying like crazy, and they even love to share your product or service with their friends.

Sounds great, right?

Falling in Love

Imagine what your business would be like if you actually fell in love with your prospect? And if you really are in love with them, wouldn't that mean you must do what's in their best interest? Sometimes this means no sale—but other times it means you must do everything in your power to get them to buy because you know the positive results they'll have.

If you love your prospect, you would be doing them a disservice to not get them to purchase. It's a subtle difference from a consultative sale, but it is dra‑matic—almost evangelical.

Again, if there's true love with the product or service, that also creates a higher-level engagement with your customers/members/clients.

On the lowest level, customers are simply getting a need met. Your product or service is their solution, so it's transactional. But with an Evolved Enterprise, there is a community being built with a true identity tied in. And at the highest level, your customers see it as their responsibility to actually "convert" others.

That's the kind of fervent identity you want to foster and create. When Mavericks did a motorcycle ride and Q&A with Rich Teerlink, former CEO of Harley Davidson, he freely admitted that having a cult-like following was one of the main reasons they could survive their dramatic marketplace downturn.

Is there a way to create this? Yes and no...

Some of it has to happen naturally, and some we can actually engineer.

As social creatures, we originated in tribal types of societies, but there's not just one chief anymore. Our loyalties are based around our multiple interests, passions, and identities.

Tribes today are more readily formed around countries, causes, religions, passions and interests, bands, wines, neighborhoods, fraternities and sororities, communities, sports teams, clubs, etc. And, of course, brands that you love and identify with.

Basically, think of these tribes or communities as cubbyholes in our brains. There are only a certain number of cubbyholes in your mind. The classic marketing read *Positioning* by Jack Trout and Al Ries really hits on this. A well-worn example is that when you think about pizza, many people would still mention Dominos.

However, your brand is no longer what you put out there—it's what other people are saying about you. That's where it gets interesting...

Swiss psychologist Carl Jung did a lot of work on archetypes. The easiest way to think about archetypes are the exaggerated characters you might see on movies and TV shows. Somebody is the jester, the caregiver, the creator, the hero, etc.

Going back to Harley, they're the outlaw archetype, even though their market is really more about white collared execs that want to be outlaws. Burning Man is about creation and self-expression. The Red Hat Society, a group of thousands and thousands of women over 50, represents the jester of just having fun. Tough Mudder is the hero brand and so on.

Brands represent lifestyle.

This actually comes back to another psychologist, Abraham Maslow. Maslow's most famous theory is his hierarchy of needs, in which people start at the bottom with fundamental security needs and then work their way up to self-actualization.

With forethought, we allow and enhance an identity tied into the customer's fullest expression of themselves.

"I am a _____."

You want to change the conversation so your tribe would actually fill in this sentence with their identity attached to you.

For instance, "I am a <u>Trekkie</u>," "I am a <u>Burner</u>," or "I am a <u>Tedster</u>."

Maverick member Damien Zamora actually told me he wants his gravestone to read: *"Here Lies a Maverick."* To me, that's the ultimate identity. He and his wife, Nikki, actually got married on a Maverick annual summit. It was a surprise engagement turned into a wedding with our musical guest, Pato Banton, marrying them off. This showcases how much members look at their community as a true family.

Years ago you might show your identity with a bumper sticker on your car. Today if someone is willing to put a sticker of your logo on their phone or iPad, you win. That means you've got a strong identity and engaged community. I'm always so pleased when I see Maverick members whip out their phones with Maverick skins on them or walking around with their branded gear.

Community Decoder #1: Origin story

From ancient times right up to the present day, stories have held readers and listeners spellbound. A well-crafted story has an almost magical ability to engage someone's emotions and get them engrossed in the message you're delivering. You can use stories to motivate action without triggering the defenses that normally come up.

And we all have a "creation story," but few of us use them in our marketing or even bother sharing.

Think of it like a comic book character.

If I asked you, "Who was bitten by a radioactive spider and started fighting crime to avenge his uncle's death?" you'd probably know this was Spider-Man.

Every business, brand, or personality has an origin story already, just waiting to be shared with the world. It's like a precious gem sitting in the attic that very few people bother to dust off and polish.

Clif Bar is a $100M+ business, and the founder, Gary Erickson, talks about going on a 175-mile bike ride, and he couldn't stomach another Powerbar. He decided to go home and concoct a better, all-natural energy bar. And as they say—the rest is history. (Even smarter, the team at Clif goes on an epiphany ride each year to relive the story. This ritual embeds the creation story into the company's culture over and over again.)

Think about your own creation story.

- **How did you start your business?**
- **What was your inspiration?**
- **What is the reason you do business the way you do?**
- **What "wrong" did you want to right?**
- **What were the obstacles you had to overcome?**

Share this with your customers, and you'll create a deeper connection.

My friend Andy Nulman, author of *Pow! Right Between the Eyes,* calls these "Velcro" connections. He started his book by revealing 10 surprising things about himself, and it really bonds the reader. One of the facts was he's a hockey goalie, and I reached out to him because we both play.

One interesting community to look at is the Red Hat Society of women ages 50+. Their origin story started on a girl's trip, when the founder, Sue Ellen Cooper, paid $7 for a red fedora hat. She bought it as a lark to give as a present along with a poem by Jenny Joseph with the opening lines:

> "When I am an old woman I shall wear purple
> With a red hat that doesn't go and doesn't suit me."

Sue gave away a few more birthday gifts of red hats along with the poem and then held an informal tea party with the idea to just have some fun as who you are. This turned into this movement with 40,000 different Red Hat Societies all across the world now.

People want to know that origin story of your brand, or what you developed, or how it was created. Here are five formulas I've used before:

1. **SERENDIPITOUS SURROUNDINGS:**
TOMS shoes' story of Blake in Argentina and just being in the right place at the right time is an example of this formula.

2. **HAPPY ACCIDENT:**
Sue Ellen Cooper's happy accident of buying the big red fedora turned into a vast community of incredible women.

3. **WHOA! PEOPLE LOVE US:**
Innocent Drinks in the UK is a perfect example of this story formula. Here's how they talk about their company's creation on their site:

We started innocent in 1999 after selling our smoothies at a music festival. We put up a big sign asking people if they thought we should give up our jobs to make smoothies, and put a bin saying 'Yes' and a bin saying 'No' in front of the stall. Then we got people to vote with their empties. At the end of the weekend, the 'Yes' bin was full, so we resigned from our jobs the next day and got cracking. (innocent-drinks.co.uk/us/our-story)

4.   **I'M MAD AS HELL, AND I'M NOT GOING TO TAKE IT:**
Gary Erickson's Epiphany ride fits the bill here of being so fed up that he had to find a better solution, which led to Clif Bars.

5.   **SCRATCH MY OWN ITCH:**
So many companies are started because the founder couldn't find exactly what they wanted in the marketplace. Maverick1000 was born out of that frustration for me. As a successful entrepreneur, I founded Maverick 1000 after being a member of many other CEO groups, masterminds, and peer-to-peer networks left me a bit flat. I simply couldn't find an organization that combined everything I wanted to not only grow my companies but also bring more joy, happiness, and greater meaning into my life.

If you want to dig deeper into this topic, you can watch a free replay of my presentation: "How to Uncover the Irresistible 'Origin' Story That Will Inevitably Attract a Following of Impassioned Fans Who Are Eager to Evangelize Your Brand" plus more on the 5 different fill-in-the-blank story formulas and a PDF workbook.
Grab it here: EvolvedEnterprise.com/resources.

Community Decoder #2: Language

It's critical that you develop your own unique and specific language for the community. Lady Gaga has her "Little Monsters," and that's on purpose, just like the KISS Army. In fact, Gene Simmons is the ultimate man at getting the KISS brand everywhere. They literally have licensed everything from KISS condoms to caskets. It's just amazing! When he was coming up with the logo, he said, "I want a logo that is easy for people to scratch into their desk at school."

Create your own internal language for the community to use.

For our community, we have **Maverick Mondays**™, which are random, crazy occurrences happening on Mondays, like surprise zombie bar crawls. Or we talk about creating **Maverick Mayhem** on the adventure days or 3X Retreats. We've coined **Maverick Multipliers**™ for business breakthroughs.

By developing more and more of your own unique language, it starts to build a little bit of an "us vs. them" type of distinction. You might remember the old Apple ads, "I'm Apple, I'm PC," showing two different types of people.

You can create a common enemy in a way based on what you stand for and what you don't, for example, Mini Coopers against big SUVs. The guys from Tough Mudder are all about "marathons are boring," and so them being against regular marathons is how they originally started. Even better is if your common enemy is something huge that you want to see changed, like Beyond Meat and their quest to battle the idea that meat is only from animals.

Community Decoder #3: Creeds

Creeds continue to solidify what your community is about. It can refine "who's in; who's out?" It can be totally objective, or it can be subjective. We have objective and subjective criteria for Maverick. It can be that if you bought something, then you are automatically in—like Jeep owners.

Your job is to attract and at the same time to repel by saying who this is not for. One way is to create a compelling manifesto declaring your values. Lululemon has theirs all over the familiar red and white bags, and it is deeply ingrained into the company ethos.

Another athletic clothing company that tackles the creed a little differently is Lorna Jane. With just three words—*move, nourish, believe*—they set the stage for what they believe in. Lorna Jane is an Australian brand just starting to make in-roads in the U.S. and other international expansion. But when I talked to the manager at the Santa Monica location, she told me they outsold Nike by a considerable margin Down Under. What I really love about the brand was the way they were looking at blending retail and a live, in-person experience (Decoder #8). Each morning, customers can gather up in the store for a chance to live and experience their values. (movenourishbelieve.com)

How about a few more you might not have seen...

The Undeclared for Life Manifesto was developed by Emile Wapnick, who helps people with multiple varied interests, declaring, "You're a Puttypeep." A Puttypeep is if you have multiple talents and you never wanted to do only one thing. Now she has a name for it, and people identify with it. (puttylike.com)

Or how about this—there's a small non-profit called Shark Angels, which is a community about saving sharks. And if you are part of this community, then their creed delivers what you are expected to do, from actions like give sharks a chance, never consume shark products, get shark smart, etc. (sharkangels.org/get-involved/duties-angels)

Community Decoder #4: Barriers and Hurdles

In one of my favorite books, *Influence: The Psychology of Persuasion*, Robert Cialdini mentions, "Persons who go through a great deal of trouble or pain to attain something tend to value it more highly than persons who attain the same thing with a minimum of effort."

Navy Seals are probably one of the toughest groups in the world to get into. And not surprisingly, these guys also have one of the tightest cohesive bonds in the world because it is such a tough organization to qualify for. Marines, Special Forces, Green Berets, etc., they all fit this type of elite groups, and you can start using this to your advantage too.

Being exclusive, like the TED conference, with a really hard ticket to get, can develop high-level ties. But it doesn't have to be about pricing. You can also set up free communities and keep the hurdles based on another criteria.

Fiskers is a 200-plus-year-old scissor and crafting company. They have developed a community of people who are deep into scrapbooking and crafts. They call them "Fiskateers," and they act as ambassadors in the crafting world, regardless of whose supplies they mention. (Fiskateers.com)

Community Decoder #5: Insider Disclosure

I believe in showcasing the good, the bad, and the ugly to really connect with your audience. On my blogs, you might see stories about when I first met my business champion, Sir Richard Branson, my kids, my proudest business accomplishments, etc.

And you'll also see me dressing up in a chicken suit to go skydiving, watch videos of me running over orange safety cones while F1 racing, and even hear the story of me falling out of my attic. (Yes, unfortunately it's a true story.)

You get the whole picture and not just the parts that make me look good. In today's world, you need to remove the spin on everything that only makes you look good.

Part of this is being an "insider."

You can give your customers this advantage in different ways, and the quirky New England-based **Johnny Cupcakes** understands this quite well. They've built their business on limited edition t-shirts, accessories, and apparel. Johnny Cupcakes has been approached numerous times by bigger retailers to have their designs in the stores—but so far they've said no. I believe that's one of the biggest reasons they remain authentic to who they are and who their customers are. Many cult brands cater to outliers, and their customers appreciate the fact they know about them and not just "everybody" can have/wear/own what they do.

You can reward your customers for being customers and make them feel like insiders too with special sales, opportunities, and announcements only for them. **Despair.com** does this with their annual BLACKOUT sale. They let customers know that anyone visiting the site that is not a customer with insider access will not be able to get into the site at all. It'll just be a big black page with no way to get in. The have special sale pricing—but only for insiders.

Community Decoder #6: Rituals

If you're a Red Wings hockey fan, you know they chuck out an octopus on the ice as a long-standing tradition during the playoffs.

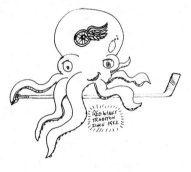

And from the other side of the world, the All Blacks rugby teams from New Zealand have a dance the fans love called the Haka that they do before the game. Essentially, it's based on a Māori war dance. It's a pretty badass ritual if ever you see a video of this. (On my Life list is to dance the Haka with the All Blacks, so if you can make it happen, let me know.)

Have you ever heard of or seen the "Jeep wave"? I borrowed my buddy's wrangler and he told me specifically, "When you take the car out, you have to wave." I said, "I don't get it." "It's the Jeep wave, and you have to do it." And the cooler the Jeep is, the more you get the wave going on. It's serious stuff with Jeep forums that even talk about the rules of the Jeep wave.

When new Maverick members join, we have a specific ritual that may or may not involve industrial strength plastic wrap and a green pill, but that's all I can say about it.

Rituals absolutely tie your community together. Start thinking about what you can do at certain steps in a customer journey from first inauguration to anniversaries or special acknowledgements.

Community Decoder #7: Artifacts

Artifacts are tangible pieces that identify some-body as part of a community.

The Livestrong yellow bracelets are one of the most popular artifacts, with bracelets everywhere. People identified with this idea of living strong and standing up to cancer in some way.

Maverick members sometimes get equipped with green mustaches when we go out. These moustaches get more attention than almost anything else we've ever done. They're silly and a bit goofy—a little bit like me.

The charity **Falling Whistles** has done a great job of creating an arti-fact that ties directly into their mission. They sell necklaces that have whistles on them and that practically force conversations from others.

The whistles are reminders of the children involved in the war in the Congo that are too small to hold guns but would have a whistle to alert their side to the enemy coming. (fallingwhistles.com/store/)

Another notion of artifacts is how do community members earn them? Your Harley leather jacket is more valuable in the group with patches from different rides and places.

Our hog riders might not want to hear this, but their jackets aren't all that dissimilar from the Boy Scouts or Girl Scouts merit badges.

There's not that much new here; it's just how you apply it.

You can keep it fun like one community of ladies called "Sisters on the Fly." This group of women will take Airstream trailers out on adventures across the country. They've also created their own merit badges, but instead of the traditional ones, they have ones with more personality, like the martini badge, the peeing outside badge, and even the nymph badge!

What other artifacts could someone earn?

Even a simple t-shirt holds rank in a community if they had to put effort in to receive it. There was a fitness program called Insanity on a lot of infomercials, and the only way you got a t-shirt was if you went through the entire program and showed the results. (Don't miss the fact that this is also a great way of gathering testimonials and customer success stories.)

For Maverick members, we have a highly coveted green Speedo.

Seriously.

The history of the Maverick Speedo is totally organic and random, which I think is the best thing sometimes. There was a husband and wife who presented me with a green Speedo at one of our events. It makes sense since they owned a large swimwear ecommerce site. The Speedo even had my initials embroidered on it and proudly proclaimed "Maverick" on the backside.

"Thank you" was all I could muster, but I didn't think I'd wear it. It's tough to rock a Speedo; you either have to be really out of shape or in amazing shape. I don't know if there's an in between. However, I thought I'd randomly pack it for the next adventure we were doing and see what happened.

That next Maverick experience was a racing event to break 200 mph driving super exotics on an airstrip we rented. Now, you couldn't go all the way up the runway; you had to make a turn at 75 to 80 miles an hour and then get on the other side and try to get to 200. It sounds exciting, but it's not quite as cool as it sounds. When you get to about 170 mph, all you're really doing is hoping that you don't run out of runway before you go off into the Everglades there.

I decided it would be funny to wear my Speedo underneath my gear. Not the best idea. Just trust me on this: It's pretty uncomfortable having a Speedo instead of underwear.

After training with the cars all day, everyone got three chances to break the 200 mph speed barrier. The first two times I didn't do it, and so I loudly proclaimed to everyone, "I need to get more aerodynamic."

That's when I literally stripped off all my clothes down to my Speedo. I put my racing helmet back on and slipped back into my car. The pro driver in the passenger seat did a serious double take and asked, "What the hell is wrong with you?"

But you can't argue with results—this time I hit 200 mph!

So now it has become part of our legend and lore. And you can't buy it—you must earn it for lifetime service. Whatever that means. Members proudly wear it, and believe it or not, it comes out at random times.

Community Decoder #8: Bigger Mission

This piece will loop back into our next section on culture too.

As humans, we're wired to want to be part of something even bigger than what we usually experience in our day-to-day lives. It's just natural human behavior. In Dan Pink's great book, *Drive*, he talks about how people are driven by three things: autonomy, mastery, and purpose. When you provide purpose for them, it serves a bigger mission. At the same time, customers are driven by the fact that they're part of something bigger too. It gets everybody involved and excited to be driving toward a bigger purpose.

When John F. Kennedy declared, "We choose to go to the moon," that inspired the whole nation to say that's where we're going.

One of my friends, Tim Schmidt, founded the U.S. Concealed Carry Association. He's used a mission to help rally his members. "We're on a mission. I need your help to make it happen. My mission is to teach 1 million people, equip 250,000 members, stop 5,000 crimes, and save 250 lives." That's a powerful scorecard for him to use with his members and team as a way of them stepping up for something big.

Provide your customers and community with something big that they can strive for together.

Community Decoder #9: Exceptional Experiences

I think experiences more than anything else really bond a community together. There's nothing better, and people are so hungry for in-person connections. Plus, the more exceptional or intense the experience, the tighter that bond is going to be. We're all craving this, no matter how many "friends" you have on Facebook. It's just not the same.

Jeep has been really smart with their popular Jeep Jamboree. They do them in multiple locations, and you simply show up there for a true experience with cool things to do with fellow Jeep enthusiasts.

Festivals have been getting bigger and bigger. Vans ended up taking over the Warped Tour because they knew that was their demographic, and it was their best way of intimately reaching that segment. Locally, around me, there's the Sweet Life Festival, which is put on by a food company that believes in truly creating a community.

And, of course, this is what we do in a big way with Maverick1000 with a bit of "Maverick Mayhem." Maverick members have blasted through the Baja, experienced a zero-gravity flight (like NASA astronauts do to prepare for space travel), flown MiG jets in Russia, climbed into the ring in Detroit's infamous 8 Mile with boxing legends and so much more. Members love the experiences as it gets them out of their normal environment.

And if you want to up the experiences even more, add elements of surprise and mystery to make it even more fun and exciting. We surprise members by taking them to dinner via snowmobile to a secluded peak in the mountains. Or springing Flashback Proms on them at Camp Maverick.

I just found something the other day called Surprise Cinema, which has been blowing up in Eastern Europe. People don't know what movie they are going to see, and they just show up and see the movie.

Add more fun to what you're doing, and then make sure you really love your community.

A great example is Keith Urban, country music star. He has a club called the Keith Urban 100 Club of super fans who have been to 100 of his concerts. That's freaking crazy!

I know fans used to follow the Dead like that, and I bet there are definitely people who hit 100 concerts, but 100 Keith Urban concerts? Keith flew all of them out to Chicago on his dime and gave them special gear (artifacts). Do you think that these people loved him even more now? Of course. And he got a ton of publicity in the country music world for that.

Measuring Your Community Score

One of the best measurement tools is called the "Net Promoter Score" (NPS). It essentially boils down to just one question you ask your customers: "How likely is it that you would recommend our company/product/service to a friend or colleague?"

Then the scoring is based on a 0–10 scale. People that respond with a score of 9 or 10 give you +1 and are your promoters, and detractors are those that respond with a score of 0 to 6, giving you a -1. Then scores of 7 or 8 are passive and count as 0. NPS is calculated by subtracting the percentage of customers that are detractors from the percentage of customers that are promoters. *Harvard Business Review* has called it the "One Number You Need to Grow." The first time we scored Maverick members, we had a +73, which was world class on par with Google and Apple. And then after actively adding even more of these Community elements, our score was +91. This is totally off the charts!

GoRuck Brand Fanatics Case Study

Let's put all these elements together with a pretty new brand that has been blowing up and really doing this right. At a recent Maverick event, we had the founder of GoRuck, Jason McCarthy, come in to present on what he's been able to build. I was really intrigued by their model after seeing this quote in **Bloomberg Business**:

"McCarthy is simultaneously building a brand and a legion of rabid, if exhausted, brand fanatics."

Here's how this fits Community Code 2.0:

Origin Story: 9/11 happened. Jason wanted to do something for his country. He enrolled into the Army and went into the special services as a Green Beret. After leaving the service, he realized from his experience that there wasn't a great rucksack out there. He just wanted to sell great bags made in the U.S. (This is a key part because he aligned with, in his words, the biggest brand he could, which was America.)

Then the origin story continued with the Tough Mudder. He talked to the organizers and had a bunch of Green Beret buddies get over there to show how tough the bags were. They decided to put bricks inside the rucksack and do the Tough Mudder. It was mostly an excuse for them to go hang out and drink beer.

He still wasn't selling many bags but realized the experience was the thing. So often our true success lies perpendicular to where we think it is. It's just like Twitter taking one tiny aspect of their previous software and turning it into something big. GoRuck correctly recognized it was about creating experiences.

Language: If you do one of their events, you're part of the class number, and your Cadre is actually an ex-Green Beret guy who comes in and trains you. There are different names for the different challenges and events.

Creed: This is something Jason calls "Good Living." GoRuck's mission statement, "Challenge excellence and do right by people," has turned into this: "It's about what we love, people, USA manufacturing, the military, local pride, dogs, and the finer things in life like beer."

Hurdles: People can relate to that and get behind that, but he's built this incredible deal: Barriers and Hurdles. These GoRuck challenges are tough; it's like 12 hours of extreme challenges. The whole deal is you have to finish as a team, and you've got to support the team. It's not a race; it's just the team creating these cohesive units. That's why you're the class of XX.

Inside Access: On their blog, Jason also has complete transparency on sales and metrics. He will show stats from their explosive growth, and that's exactly what happens when you have a great community. He'll also share the truth about their goofs and pitfalls.

Rituals: They have something called the "Welcome Party," which is straight out of his Green Beret training. In fact, Jason took a lot of this stuff about creating cohesive units from his service. The Welcome Party is a bunch of push-ups, flutter kicks, army carries, and high-stepping formation marching. All good stuff, but now add 40 lbs. of bricks in your backpack.

For Mavericks, our Welcome Party started at midnight. Yep, we actually did a GoRuck challenge in the streets of DC, trekking through the mall with nobody else around. It was really something else and ended with a well-deserved beer directly across from the White House eight hours later.

Artifacts: You cannot get a GoRuck patch any other way except by completing your mission. It is not for sale. As they say on the site, it takes inspiration from first special forces spearhead. What's more, they've created ascension because there are additional advanced challenges you can participate in. Now that's an advanced strategy of showing your customers what to do or where to go next.

Bigger Mission: Jason and GoRuck are all about the Green Beret Foundation, which serves Green Berets and their families, to date raising over $450,000. You better believe that community loves the fact that they do that. They tell you right up front how much money from each event or purchase goes into the Foundation.

Exceptional Experiences: GoRuck lives this. You can pretty much sign up for something happening all around you. Now, the proof is they've only been around a very, very short time; they've got tens of thousands of likes already, but even more important are the types of comments they get on social media.

"I was so glad I came into contact with your brand, I mean, our brand." When you can get that kind of ownership, you win.

GoRuck has truly turned this brand selling into so much more than a bag. The interesting thing is you need a rucksack to do the challenges. Now, it doesn't have to be one of theirs, but you better believe they sell a whole lot of them because selling the bags isn't even the main focus.

Go out and use these same Community Decoder pieces to build an amazing community as a key part of your Evolved Enterprise and a setup for the final piece...

CULTURE

— PETER DRUCKER

 **CHAPTER TEN**

WHY CULTURE IS CRITICAL

If you had shown me this chapter a few years ago, I probably would have laughed in your face. You see, I previously thought company culture was a waste of resources—today I know that's absolutely wrong!

In fact, with exactly five minutes left on an off-site kick-off for Maverick, I remember asking our team, "So what kind of culture do you want?" Ha. That's how much of my mindshare it used to receive—but not anymore.

I've come a long way in realizing the importance of culture.

Perhaps what really baffled me was that culture is something you can't always put your finger on. It's not totally tangible, and you don't necessarily see it on your P&L. Whether it's implicit or explicit, there's always a culture in any organization.

I've been fortunate now to have been friends with and had meaningful conversations with all sorts of individuals I really admire for the way they've created an exceptional culture in their companies. And they've had a profound influence on my thoughts here.

I believe it's now a law that you cannot have a business book that mentions culture without including Tony Hsieh and Zappos. (I kid. I kid.) Fact is, I'm truly inspired by his vision and how he's been able to build Zappos up to $1B+ in sales before selling to Amazon. (So I guess you can put Culture on your P&L.) Actually, I was just in Vegas checking out Tony's new Airstream park community living project that's one tiny piece of his Downtown Project. Yes, he actually lives in an airstream trailer. Tony is always experimenting with new ways to create community and "collisions," as he calls them. The night I was there, we had a random assortment of high-tech CEOs, new media experts, social innovators, and random "neighbors" all cooking food together. And in most cases, you don't know who's who.

Tony spoke at our Underground® seminar for two years in a row as a keynote, and throughout his presentation, he harped on delivering WOW! He said culture is your #1 priority—so much so that Zappos spends four weeks training new team members and even offers them $4,000 now to leave instead of staying. That's a big deal. They do so much with culture it's hard to even put it all into one spot.

Tony would keep telling me and other Mavericks that you must be willing to not just hire for core values but actually fire for them too. That means they need to be meaningful and not just something that looks good on a plaque inside your office. For instance, one of Zappos' 10 core values is "Be Humble." One sneaky test was to ask the shuttle driver how a prospective employee treated them on the ride in from the airport. And if it wasn't respectfully, they wouldn't get offered a job, no matter how much of a superstar they might seem to be.

Learning from Tony and Zappos, we have evolved our core values three times now. Here's the first set:

Maverick Core:

Maverick companies embody the internal and external philosophy of **'Make More Money, Have More Fun, and Give More'**. Business bliss and balance are found where all 3 connect.

Maverick DNA:

1. **A Little Bit Quirky, a Little Bit Rock n' Roll** - not taking ourselves too seriously while having something pretty damn frickin' cool going on!

2. **C'mon Baby Light My Fire** - creating the spark & connection for successful entrepreneurs.

3. **But Wait, There's More...** Obviously taken from a typical infomercial line, this is a driving goal of creating surprise, delight and astonishment beyond expectations.

4. **Ripple** – Maverick is not just a pebble thrown in a pond, but a boulder. We create massive impact with our charitable and philanthropic innovation, entrepreneurship and giving forward.

5. **Banish the Ordinary.** Why have an ordinary life or create an ordinary business? You make the rules and that's what we're all about.

We weren't applying this and integrating into the company, so we scrapped it. And the second time around, I thought we really hit on what we wanted. It looked like this:

Maverick DNA Core Values

Multipliers
Creative focus on finding leverage points for the critically few *"little hinges that swing big doors"* to accelerate exponential results and value

Astonishment Architecture™
For any product category or service, there is an expected level of satisfaction and value by the end user. Our job is to astonish at each point of contact or interaction. **But wait, there's more…**this is a driving goal of creating surprise, delight, and astonishment beyond expectations.

Vision for a Bigger Future
Individually and collectively growing, learning, and getting smarter… then spreading that knowledge further among the Maverick community

Extraordinary
Banish the ordinary—why have an ordinary life or create an ordinary business? You get to make the rules, decide what really matters, and determine how you keep score.

Re-Imagine, Re-Invent & Re-Create
Consistently and continually disrupting, differentiating, and innovating

Impact
Maverick is not just a pebble thrown in a pond but a boulder. We're the catalyst for massive impact with our philanthropic innovation, entrepreneurship giving forward initiatives, and scholarships.

Connect, Catalyze & Co-Create
Instigating the spark, inspiration & connection for bold 21st century entrepreneurs. And co-creating something with infinitely more value and sharing in the greater rewards with everyone at the table

Kiss Kiss, Bang Bang
A little bit quirky, a little bit rock n' roll—not taking ourselves too seriously but still being really (okay, mostly) cool even in green Speedos or an Elvis wig

It's a nice acronym out of the word MAVERICK that's gotten incorporated into the business in many ways, including having all new members repeat part of this as a creed.

But this still wasn't enough...

My team sat me down one day and said we were not living our core values internally. We were doing an excellent job providing these for our members and the outside world, but these values were not "hireable" or "fireable."

Developing your core values is something that's essential to a strong culture, and it's incredibly important that you can actually live them. Don't make them what you think they should be—but what your company really is.

Developing world-class culture takes commitment, and I was back to the drawing board again.

To get going, I'd highly recommend getting out of your office. For us as a virtual company, that meant finding a place to convene all together. Depending on the size of your company, you may want only your leadership team or everyone. We're a small team, so everyone participated. I go by the principle my buddy, Brendon Burchard, harps on: "People support what they create."

Core Values Discovery Session

I carefully set the stage for the best potential results by asking everyone to share something they were proud of in the company and that was going well. This gets the energy to a positive place first and helps us focus on leveraging our strengths. I then presented for 15 minutes on my big why and our compelling Vision. (We'll cover specifics for a great vision shortly.)

Next I had everyone go around the room to Identify and share the characteristics of their business and personal heroes. I've found that when people talk about their heroes, they typically pull out archetypes and traits that represent their best selves. Then I asked the team to actually share a specific quality they appreciate about each person, something that was a reflection of a positive value in our business.

Both of these exercises are great lead-ins to discussions of core values we have already and what we want more of. We provided everyone a list of nearly 400 different values for everyone to think about and told them to come prepared with 5–10 to share. Then we listed one value on one Post-It note and kept filling up the wall. But I set the constraint that they could only have five at first, so they had to think of the most important ones to stick up there. Then I gave them a few more to keep adding and brainstorming.

At this point, you'll start seeing repeating ideas emerge, so we can consolidate them into categories.

Then things get messier...

I let everyone cast three votes. Again there's a constraint here to get to their most important values as a priority. I allowed them to vote for one value three times if they wanted to make sure it was saved. Then I gave them another bonus vote in the next round and one more bonus vote to keep eliciting what was most important.

Next come the discussions and heated exchanges. I actually find this process incredibly worthwhile to embrace the positive conflict if it's done with respect and in the interest of a greater mission. Once we got to a manageable list, I was tasked with incubating on the notes and coming up with a draft of the new Core Values. Make sure you are capturing all of these notes with pictures so you can refer back over and over again as the process moves forward.

I woke up the next morning and quickly jotted notes down on my hotel's stationary next to my bed. Then with a bit more tweaking, I created a draft I could show the team for feedback, which finally turned into this EVOLVED acronym:

"Changing the Way Business is PLAYED"

EVERYDAY FUNDAY

VENTURE FORWARD ... (further & faster)

OPEN & REAL

LITTLE HINGES

VOTE WITH YOUR HEART

EXTRA! EXTRA!

DARE GREATLY

Here's the process recapped:

- Set the Energy with Excitement
- Inspire with Your Big WHY
- Share the Vision (draft)
- Heroes & Heroic Trait You Appreciate in Your Team Members
- List of All Values (shared ahead of time)
- One Value/One Post-It Note
- Consolidate
- Discuss
- Incubate

Since realizing the importance of culture, I have loved visiting great companies to see what they're doing so we can model bits and pieces of what's working. This past summer, Maverick members visited **Motley Fool**, ranked the #1 best medium-sized business in America to work for as rated by Glassdoor.

Motley Fool is heavily committed to their own internal team of "fools," and being ranked the #1 business by Glassdoor is pretty significant. That's because the list is compiled solely on the input of employees anonymously reviewing their workplace. The benefits are remarkable for "fools" (employees)—everything from unlimited vacations, healthy food, education, fun experiences, and even $1,000 in their own account to invest in a Fool-recommended stock upon being hired.

One of the more interesting company benefits we saw firsthand was their "Fool's Errand." They had a big board with pictures from past winners and where they've gone. From their internal blog (culture. fool.com/category/vacation-policies/):

*The Fool's Errand is a special prize—two weeks off and $1,000. So what are the rules? The chosen Fool must leave immediately and have no contact with the office, with the money only available if these guidelines are followed. The generous gift of $1,000 can be used for anything—plane tickets, hotel rooms, skydiving lessons...you name it! Past winners have visited Northern California wineries; Captiva Island, Florida; snowy Vermont; and even the Dominican Republic. Some Fools have simply enjoyed a staycation, but no matter where they go, winners are always encouraged to spend a few hours on our company's purpose—**to help the world invest better**. Winners have rebalanced their 401k, managed an educational savings account, or chatted with a parent about retirement preparation.*

Obviously, the Fool's Errand fulfills our core value of Fun, but it also fulfills two business purposes. First, even with an unlimited vacation policy, some Fools find it hard to fully disconnect from the office. We want to encourage our employees to take the occasional break. Second, it's important for any company to be prepared for an employee's sudden, unexpected absence (illnesses and family emergencies happen). By knowing that we can cover for a Fool who needs to take time off with short notice, we know there are no gaps in our workflow.

If your company would like to try a similar program, you can start small. Maybe offer a random employee a day off as a reward for great work. Show your employees that time off is important—and they'll return with fresh ideas and greater motivation.

Regardless if you set an intentional culture or not, there's always a culture within your company.

Your employees could be showing up just for their paycheck at the lowest level of engagement or at the highest level because they truly believe they're playing a part in something bigger.

And what if your goal as the leader was to help everyone on your team become the fullest expression of themselves? Same as your personal evolution, right? Your company can be the container and catalyst for growth, learning, and complete expression of their gifts and talents. Not everyone is wired to do their own thing, but when you can give your team a "sandbox" to build their dreams, they win and you win.

On our team, we start with strengths testing and then, through some trial and error, help members experiment and move into the roles best suited for them—hopefully ones they're totally charged up about—and it makes a big difference.

Previous studies have shown that 70% of workers are either not engaged or actively disengaged—meaning they are actively trying to sabotage your business. And actually, new numbers I've seen from Gallup show this percentage is increasing to 87%. It's your duty to allow everyone to show up as their greatest selves and bring their full heart and soul to your venture.

And they'll go above and beyond if you let them. I just got a note from a new Team Green member saying she was offered two times her current salary with us to return to her previous employer. She turned him down flat because of the deep alignment to what we are doing. That's the power of intentional culture and an Evolved Enterprise. And here's another note I received:

"I just want to say thank you for listening to my ideas and giving me the space to grow them. I have never experienced this type of freedom in my job and cannot even begin to express how much it means to me. I am very passionate about working toward positive change in our world. There is nothing I aspire to more than to be in a place where I can really help people. So once again, thank you for giving me the opportunity to realize my dreams. I love Maverick—the team and the members."

The Culture of Joy

Menlo Innovations (menloinnovations.com) in Ann Arbor Michigan, is a really intriguing example of living and embodying culture. They design and build custom software for high-end clients -- but they decided that they were not going to do anything in the company unless in resulted in more joy. More joy for their team, their clients and even their community.

And their CEO, Richard Sheridan, has recently written a wonderful book called *Joy, Inc.* that digs deep into their culture. They wanted to free up engineers to do their best work they had to do things differently, like taking away the fear of estimating wrong, creating open workspaces, no ambiguity about exactly what they would be working on and so much more.

But one of their biggest innovations is "pairing".

This is having two people work together on the same task. Most companies would see this as a waste of resources but not here. This promotes collaboration on ideas, peer accountability, and cross-pollination of project knowledge.

In a recent Forbes interview, Sheridan stated, "Pairing is the most powerful managerial tool ever discovered. It makes so many things change, and change rapidly. The fact that we assign the pairs and switch them every five days, and sometimes sooner, this creates a human energy that is unstoppable."

Just like Zappos and Zingermans, you can visit Menlo Innovations and tour the facility and learn exactly what they're doing there to elicit so much joy.

Growth from Culture

Rich Teerlink, former CEO of Harley Davidson, has said, "People are your only sustainable competitive advantage." And that's the exact same quote my friend John Ratliff has told a small group of different high-level business owners repeatedly over the five years he's been part of our trips together to Necker Island. The funny thing is John had never seen Rich say this or even knows about this quote. Great minds truly do think alike.

My buddy John founded Appletree Answers in 1995 from his two-bedroom apartment and grew it through a number of acquisitions to 24 locations and 650 employees before selling it in 2012. I've never seen anyone at the ground level so passionate about making the lives of his employees better and living/breathing the culture.

It showed up in the company's growth and in a reduction of employee turnover from the average of 100% to just 18% between 2008 and 2012 by using a key initiative called "Dream On." Think of this as Make-A-Wish but for employees.

I remember John literally crying as he shared the story with us of a team member who wanted to have her husband, who was suffering through cancer, to get a VIP treatment to see a Philadelphia Eagles football game. Well, John's team at Appletree did one better. Through connections they had, they were able to set up a meeting with the husband's favorite Eagles player for autographs and pics. It was magical.

Appletree is the best I've seen at taking a commodity-like business and integrating a culture of caring. The company actually won the "We Love Our Workplace" video contest, run by the prestigious Great Place to Work Institute, in 2012. And all of this translated into getting 11x what most other companies in this industry get as a valuation.

The Giving Experiment

Giving away money to cause partners to raise employee performance might sound counterintuitive, but Listen Trust (formerly Listen Up Español), headed up by two of our Maverick1000 members, proves this works. Strategic giving when done with intention can provide a significant ROI for everyone.

From 2008 to 2011 the company experienced a 123% growth rate and currently generates around $14 million in revenue per year. In late 2011 they tested and successfully demonstrated that charitable gifts can be used to motivate employee performance. Here's how President Tony Ricciardi describes what they did in an email to me:

Two of our core values are Going Beyond Ourselves and Growing Braincells. Our original goal was to figure a way to increase our 3rd party upsells of free trial membership after we close the sale that the person was calling in on. We thought that if we tied a charity aligned with our core passions it would motivate the agents to have a higher pitch rate and conversion of these offers, which sometimes make the calls unusually long. Our thought was if we tie the sale of these programs to a charity outside just commission; then the agents are offering it to support something bigger than just a commission.

I do not know the exact lift in sales conversions to these programs [it was 17%], but it was a positive impact to the "Happiness Factor" in the call center and gave agents and the staff something of greater importance to talk about other than our Call Center KPIs.

The Charity give I think has to be big enough to get the call center rallied around. The company sponsored international school builds, where we would send 10 people to do it and we would have it video documented to share with the entire company at the annual Christmas party. (We recognized not everyone can go on a school build trip; however, everyone had a hand in making it possible, and we wanted them to see what they helped us achieve.) We also support a school in Chicago outside the school build—the school population in Chicago is about 2,000 kids, 98% 1st and 2nd generation Mexican Americans. We partner with Buildon.org to manage an after-school program where it allows the kids to work on community service programs. We have found that when kids are in a less than desirable atmosphere and are put in situations to help people less fortunate than them, it empowers them to do more and ignites a fire of confidence. So we see higher attendance, graduation, and college advancement with the kids enrolled in this program. We document this program every year as well and share it with the center— this ties in with the affinity of Mexicans helping Mexican Americans break the cycle of trying to enculturate into the U.S. economy.

Tying the vision of acting on your passions and sharing the results back to your workforce is a feel good of Listen Up Español. We are one of the lucky companies that have reaped the benefit in creating it and experiencing it. Lastly, our clients like to hear the story of what we are doing along with our partners. It says something about who we are, and it is a great story other than what we do day in and day out—it makes us different and interesting. (Sort of like being a Maverick.)

Notice that the charity aligns with their core values while at the same time getting both the employees and the customers involved. The upsell gets customers to buy more frequently with revenue from this product donated to charity. Working with buildOn, the charity ties in directly with Listen Trust's core values. As Tony has been quoted before, "Most companies miss this point. The key is the connection—the company has to connect the charity give to the personal or company passions."

CEO Craig Handley has the vision for something even greater. He said the team set "a goal to give a billion dollars to charity. We knew we had to be creative in how we did it, and we wanted charitable giving to work for us."

How Core Values Dictate Decisions and New Ideas

Craig is one of the most big-hearted and creative people I know. After being inspired by Zappos' culture on a field trip we took together, he had a brainstorm of giving away a car. The deal was they would give away a new car every other month to the best-performing sales agents. Sounds like a good idea, right?

After a year (and six cars given away), they sent out a survey to ask employees about the cleanliness, the temperature in the building, the security, the lighting, the management, the pay, the incentives, the likelihood that they'd leave if another company offered them more money, etc. The survey across the board showed an improvement in all areas just because of a focus on core values. You would think this is a great idea, but it didn't fully line up with the company's core values.

When Listen Trust created their core values with their team, one of them was "United as One." And team members shared their concern that winning a car was great, but it was only great for one person. Plus, the majority of the team, including the top performers, didn't feel it fully lined up around another core value of "living life like an extreme sport." With this new feedback (based on core values), they stopped giving away the car and provided a broader selection of incentives to get as many employees as possible to benefit.

I want you to notice what really happened here. A big benefit of living your culture and core values is that they are used as the touchstone for what should be done, not some arbitrary notion of "do what I say." And anyone on the team can call anyone else out, including the CEO, by using the core values as their measuring stick. With our new core values in place, that's happened multiple times in regard to how we make decisions and what we do in the different companies.

Two Bonus Evolved Enterprise Culture Chapters

Evolved Enterprise is a movement to change the way business is played taking place with multiple voices. These bonus chapters provide additional real-world perspectives of what's working from the community.

Bonus Chapter #1: "How to SHIFT Your Culture" contributed by Maverick1000 member and culture expert, Joe Mechlinski. Joe and his team at entreQuest are some of the best in the world at working with mission-driven companies to help them create a culture that creates a competitive advantage. He is a New York Times best-selling author, speaker, entrepreneur, and community activist. Named one of Maryland's Most Admired CEOs and Finalist for Ernst of Young Entrepreneur of Year, Joe has helped more than 500 companies (including his own) prosper through some of the worst economic times in history...and it all starts with culture.

Bonus Chapter #2: "Cultivate a Culture of Growth" contributed by Dmitriy Kozlov on the intersection of culture and operations. We met when he won a scholarship to our Underground® seminar and now he's evolved into helping me release Evolved Enterprise into the world and co-founding Maverick NEXT together. The lessons Dima shares here come primarily from experience building his agency, Vision Tech Team, to over 30 passionate team members in two years along with the direct consulting to his agency's clients (who are all top thought leaders) and the exceptional young entrepreneurs in Maverick NEXT. As a millennial himself, his experience is insightful here for recruiting, retaining, and developing an extraordinary to scale your organization's impact.

Download the bonus chapters at:
EvolvedEnterprise.com/resources

CHAPTER ELEVEN

YOUR ENGAGING VISION

The big elephant in the room is the startling statistic that 70% of the workplace is not actively engaged in their work. Think about this for a moment. You've no doubt seen this, or maybe even experienced it yourself, when you just "phone it in." The company that can truly win the hearts and souls of their team excels.

How do you do that? (Hint: The chapter on Community Code 2.0 also works for your team.)

Providing the Vision

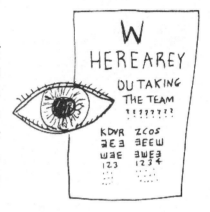

Your team wants something bigger that they're working for too. Creating a compelling and inspiring vision and mission is the key to making sure you get where you want to go and that your team is behind you. This is also how you know what to say "Yes" to and, more importantly, what to say "No" to.

Quite frankly, when I first got started in business, I thought the ideas of Visions and Mission Statements were pretty much total B.S.—just stuff that looked really good framed next to a bathroom.

But I've had two people who have greatly influenced me in this regard. The first is my friend Cameron Herold, author of *Double Double*. Cameron was the former COO of 1-800-Got-Junk and helped the company grow from $2 million to $105 million in revenue in six years with no debt or outside shareholders, an awesome achievement by any standard.

One of the "secrets" to his success is having a Vivid Vision, a document that gives a specific description of what your company looks like and "acts like" at a certain time in the future. You can get more details on his process here: cameronherold.com/vivid-vision.

And the other significant mentor in this area is Ari Weinzweig, co-founder of Zingerman's, who I mentioned when talking about Ecosystems.

Ari is loath to cite one secret for their success (and truthfully, there is never just one factor), but getting good at visioning is something they do everywhere in the organization, so there's got to be something to that:

"One of the biggest contributors to the level of creativity in our organization is the regularity with which we teach, use, and stick to the visioning process. We start pretty much every planning effort with a draft of a positive vision of the future. And we do it at every level of the organization. Whether we're working on visions for a business five years out, a project that will be done in five months, or a dinner special that will be on the menu at 5:00 tonight, we're pretty consistently 'beginning with the end in mind.'"

I have two great interviews with Ari that you can access at the resources page - EvolvedEnterprise.com/resources

Interview #1: "How to Develop Your Ideal Vision for Your Great Business and Perfect Future"

Interview #2: "Unconventional Methods for Effective Self-Management and Conscious Creativity"

In fact, it's been proven that when people use visioning instead of simply problem solving, energy levels increased, innovative ideas flowed, and people were excited and eager about their future. What's more, visioning also gets you clear on what you do NOT want to do in your business so that you can easily turn away seemingly golden opportunities that come your way. (This is why Ari and his partner always said no to creating franchises or other locations outside Ann Arbor.)

We show our Vision to everyone: current and prospective team members, partners, vendors, customers/members, etc. I want everyone enrolled and excited in where we are going.

How Do You Create That Compelling Vision?

Each time my process starts in my journal to dig deep into what really makes my heart sing and how I want to wake up excited to jump into the day. Ari recommends always starting by writing down all your "prouds"—those that you're most proud of in your business, your accomplishments, and your wins from the company. This sets a positive energy to start the process. I'd strongly suggest getting out of your office. I find water has an amazing creative effect on me, so if I can go the beach or our local river, I'm able to get some powerful pieces.

Don't edit or second-guess yourself because you think something isn't possible.

Your Vision allows you to dream and not get hung up on where your business is today but where you are going in the 3-5 year timeframe you set. Cameron recommends three years, and I would mostly agree. (Except for my most recent Vision, when we went out to 2020, which was four years because it was such a perfect date, right?)

Here's how our newest 2020 Vision starts:

2020 represents "perfect vision". It's time for Evolved Entrepreneurs, visionary creators, and Maverick leaders to rewrite the rules of business for the 21st century. Together we can co-create innovative business ideas applied to solve significant global issues.

Our goal is to instigate the instigators, connect the connectors and catalyze the catalysts—with a dash of maverick mischief thrown in.

We believe business can be the biggest lever for making a meaningful difference in the world. *Collectively, one community of impactful entrepreneurs can change the way business is played!*

The 2020 Evolved EcoVerse is a group of interconnected businesses & ventures overlaid with the *Evolved Enterprise framework* run by collaborative Profit Partners. Think of a truly thriving ecosystem, similar to an ocean reef. The whole provides an abundance of nourishment to an incredibly diverse group of organisms. And even the dead marine life around a reef provides the building blocks for the coral—just like "failed" projects or ideas build the EcoVerse with more experience, data, and insights.

What should you include?

Pretty much everything we've covered in this material should be included:

- ✓ **Your deepest reason why, cause, and mission**

- ✓ **Your impact scoreboard and measurements**

- ✓ **Who are you serving and how? That's your community and what makes you special and alluring.**

- ✓ **Your team's core values and how you help engage your team fully**

Your role is not to worry about the "how" at this point either; your job is to simply create the very specific "what" this would look and feel like if you were stepping foot into your ideal company.

What else might you include?

- **Your company size and scope. (Are you a billion dollar company or a multi-million dollar company? How many team members? Are they in-person or virtual? What's the office consist of?)**

- **What does the brand feel like? Identity/language**

- **Who are your advisors? Partnerships? Media?**

I've been re-reading our 2009 and 2012 visions as I write this chapter, and it's pretty amazing to see how much we did accomplish from each of the Visions. Not everything for sure—but more times than not, it starts showing up as real. And the essence of what I've really wanted is always there.

One smart tip from Ari is to write "DRAFT" at the top of your Vision so it doesn't hold so much sway over you. And then circulate early drafts to people you trust to provide positive and constructive input. I also really like a graphic look for my Visions, so I have my own doodles and an artist on our team to punch up some of the pieces. Do whatever makes you most excited about seeing this Vision come to life.

The next stage is truly where the magic happens.

It's in the editing process that you really start simplifying and cutting what's most important. I might edit my document a dozen times or more. Each time I'm looking to ensure it is clear and concise but also compelling. I want to make sure it's truly special and unique to us, and that it gets me super excited in a big way!

Now, once you have your final Vision, don't edit it before the date you've set.

I admit I am often tempted to tinker with it, but I leave it alone since it's more of a guidepost for everyone than anything else. I have added a sentence in our Visions that helps me feel better about this notion that something new will show up that I didn't consider:

The Evolved EcoVerse also has the unique flexibility to shift into new opportunities and projects that may not even be seen yet if they line up against the Mission, DNA, and values.

Make sure you use your Vision everywhere and don't just file it away. We refer back to the Vision when we have our quarterly strategy sessions, and I've even had team members read from it aloud.

If you'd like to see a copy of our 2020 EcoVerse Vision
and a few other examples, you can download it here:
www.EvolvedEnterprise.com/resources.

2020 Evolved EcoVerse Mission

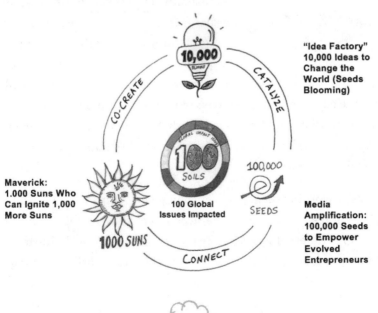

"Idea Factory" 10,000 Ideas to Change the World (Seeds Blooming)

Maverick: 1,000 Suns Who Can Ignite 1,000 More Suns

100 Global Issues Impacted

Media Amplification: 100,000 Seeds to Empower Evolved Entrepreneurs

The Heart of Your Team

I believe we need to have our team show up as their best selves and provide them a platform for optimizing their own unique expression. (In many ways, this mirrors the section on evolving "YOU.")

One of the best books I've devoured recently on this topic and the evolution of work is *Reinventing Organizations* by Frederick Laloux. He has coined the term "Teal" companies as evolutionary businesses. One of the key characteristics is that they provide space for individuals to do their own "inner work" while doing the "outer work" of the company.

To that end, one of the benefits we've introduced is a Maverick Mindfulness allocation to our team. This is a discretionary $1,000 they can use any way they want throughout the year if it provides more mindfulness, unique experiences, or development. It could be yoga classes, massages, or even taking the day off to take the kids to a water park. It's not a large

amount, but it's enough to make a difference; then the team member reports back what they did and how they felt.

As a team, we've also done "33-Day Experiments." For 33 days, we all decide on something together that we want to improve or get better at and then track our progress using a team Trello board.

One of the experiments was 33 days of random acts of kindness, and I was really touched and impressed by what many of our "Team Green" members did. The last one was writing in the five-minute journal each day to focus on gratitude.

As a leader working on actively engaging your culture, you need to decide what really is important because you might read this book and have a ton of different ideas, but we know that doesn't work. The team will simply wait it out like the last time the boss had a brilliant change of plans after attending a seminar or workshop.

You need to decide if culture is a priority or not. Consider how you are going to integrate your culture into your rhythms and routines. This is an ongoing process that is not an overnight change. Your culture will slowly evolve, but your goal is to ensure there is a way for your team to bring their full heart and soul to what they do for you. We still continue to work on this, but I know we get better and better each day.

Make Space on the Calendar

Maverick1000 member Joe Mechlinski decided that learning and growth were key focuses for his team, so they did something drastic—they literally took the last half of Fridays off every week. They figured not much really happens on Friday afternoon anyway in most cases. And instead of wasting it, they were going to make their team better.

Each Friday would be either a team learning day, a bonding activity/experience, or a "giving" day, where the team volunteered in some way. You better believe this made them smarter and stronger! Joe's secret is that you need to create the space on your calendar for growth if you're going to do it.

One of the small things that has made a difference for us during team meetings is something so simple yet really powerful. I picked this up from John Mackey, co-CEO of Whole Foods. He talks about how at the end of each meeting, they would go around the room and each person would share one or more "appreciations" for someone else there.

This has been huge.

There is a massive energy shift when individuals acknowledge someone else for a key task or just for what they're doing.

Appreciation is so powerful in many ways with all your key relationships for work and personally. And this works for everyone.

187

Missy and I play a game at dinner sometimes with the kids, where all of us go around the table and say one specific thing we appreciate about everyone.

It's really awesome to see your kids' heads pop up like little flowers as their brother or sister says something nice about them.

Now, I'd be remiss if I didn't do this too. I truly appreciate you for investing in reading and applying this material. **Most people are only too willing to stay with the status quo. It's the impactful 21st-century entrepreneurs, like you, who are willing to look at where you can make a meaningful difference through business that will help us change the way business is played.**

Thank you!

- Y.S.

Awaken

It's time for Maverick entrepreneurs, visionary creators, change makers, and impactful leaders to wake up and step fully into an accelerated entrepreneurial evolution.

What Serves the Collective Whole Also Serves You

Business is the biggest leverage for making a significant difference, and you can be a beacon for others following your path. You're being asked to step up with your talents, capabilities, and gifts to open up a new era of capitalism. You're needed as an ambassador to lift and transform the notion of what business looks like in the 21st century.

And there's nothing more exciting than someone fully engaged sharing their gifts and talents in the world. Simply allow yourself to play, experiment, and explore using joy, passion, and excitement as your barometer for what's next...

When you finally align the true soul of your business with more impact, meaning, and happiness, you'll inevitably create greater profits. This is a coming shift that will change everything.

The Evolved Enterprise concepts are now a seed planted in your consciousness with unlimited possibilities erupting forth. This germ of an idea holds the entire holographic blueprint of your greater purpose. Even if you don't exactly know HOW you're going to accomplish what you are being called to do—it doesn't matter. You don't need to know every step except the first one, and then the next, and the next again. Open up the space for your destiny to flourish, and live your legendary legacy.

I fully believe that you cannot have within you a deep, deep desire for a creation without also at the same time having the capacity, natural abilities, and resources to bring it into being.

> *"What you seek...is also seeking you."*
> —Rumi

Leave your mark as an extraordinary entrepreneur by merging your head, heart, and higher purpose...delivered through your Evolved Enterprise.

You already know the answers you need. Just don't get lost in the entire process of how you're going to get to where you want to be. Feel this new shift emerging and blossoming within yourself and your organization.

Your time is now to rewrite business as usual.

There is never a perfect time or the right conditions for planting the seed of an Evolved Enterprise. Build the damn thing already—your customers are waiting to fall in love with you!

ABOUT YANIK SILVER

Yanik Silver redefines how business is played in the 21ˢᵗ century at the intersection of more profits, more fun, and more impact.

He is the founder of Maverick1000, a private, invitation-only global network of top entrepreneurs and industry leaders. This group periodically assembles for breakthrough retreats, rejuvenating experiences, and impact opportunities (to-date raising over $3M+) with participating icons such as Sir Richard Branson, Tony Hawk, Chris Blackwell, John Paul DeJoria, Tony Hsieh, Russell Simmons, Tim Ferriss, and many others.

Yanik serves on the Constellation board for Virgin Unite, the entrepreneurial foundation of the Virgin Group and Branson family. And his lifetime goal is to connect visionary leaders and game changers to catalyze business models and new ideas for solving 100 of the world's most impactful issues by the year 2100.

In between checking off items on his Ultimate Big Life List, he calls Potomac, Maryland, home with his wife, Missy, and two mini-maverick adventurers in the making, Zack and Zoe.

That's the regular stuff. Now the more unusual material:

- ✔ He won the "Oscar Meyer Weiner" ice hockey shootout championship (twice) as a kid. His men's league team still yells "Oscar Meyer" when he infrequently gets a breakaway.

- ✔ He surprised Sir Richard Branson dressed as a showgirl in Vegas before a keynote speech.

191

- ✔ He broke 200mph in a racecar with nothing more than a green speedo on.

- ✔ He was the 4th grade lead for the Tin Woodsman in *The Wizard of Oz*, and that was the start and end of his promising theater career. (He still can sing most of his solo.)

- ✔ His birthday is 9/25, and inside sterling silver, you will often see the number .925.

- ✔ He snuck out at the age of 5 to buy markers with his Hanukah money—only to catch the wrong bus home and end up at the police station. (Undaunted, his love of doodling still continues to this day!)

Personal Blog: **YanikSilver.com**

Evolved Ecoverse of aligned companies: **MaverickDNA.com**

Twitter: **@YanikSilver**

Yanik is also available on a limited basis for select speaking and consulting engagements.

Join Up With Other Exceptional Leaders and Impactful Entrepreneurs to Collectively Amplify and Accelerate Your Business Growth and Impact

It's sounds cliché, but together we truly can achieve more...

But I don't believe "together" is just joining hands and singing "Kumbaya" around the campfire.

There's got to be a collective win for everyone involved...

...an intelligent way to create a bigger win for yourself and the group by leveraging key relationships, shared knowledge and resources, media exposure, and joint partners.

Moving toward the transcending level of an Evolved Enterprise hinges on actively engaging shared networks and collaborative partnerships.

And as one of the early advocates, here's a way for you to come together with other like-minded evolved entrepreneurs to support, magnify, and prod each other.

You're invited to become a charter member of the new **Evolved Enterprise**

Catalyst COalition...
How Being a Charter Member of the Evolved Enterprise™ Catalyst COalition Works for You:

COAMPLIFY	COCREATE	CONNECTION
• Media Exposure in National publications like *USA Today* • PR Team working to feature Evolved Enterprises • Network Effect with trustmarks and badges identifying members as an Accredited Evolved Enterprise	• Step-by-Step Evolved Enterprise Blueprint Workshop for You and Your Team • Business Model Brainstorming • "Swipe File" Reference Library of promotional ideas and impact pieces ready to model and modify.	• Member Connection to share resources, skills, and support • Link with new potential partners and joint ventures • Invitation to in-person events and gatherings

www.EvolvedEnterprise.com/catalyst

193

(Which One Will YOU Build?)

My personal lifetime goal to connect visionary leaders and game changers to co-create innovative ideas & new business models to measurably impact 100 global issues.

In order to help make a dent in those 100 issues – we have the somewhat audacious goal of catalyzing 10,000 Evolved Enterprises into the world by the year 2020. I look at the Evolved Enterprise book in your hand as a 'seed'...and then helping you plant that seed to bring 10,000 "blooms" bursting forth!

It's this driving mission that makes me want to jump out of bed in the morning, and work tirelessly to see it come together. But it's also so big, it scares the hell out of me. Yes, I "get" that it's a really gigantic, bold goal, and a lot of people might even think I am crazy to think it can be done.

To be brutally honest with you, I think it myself sometimes...

And that is REALLY good news for you, because my team and I have been working insane hours for god knows

how long to build out every system, uncover every last bit of leverage, and open every possible door to help make it happen for those who join in this goal with me.

- The partnerships with like-minded entrepreneurs who are eager to see you win.
- The access to already existing databases & channels to move your products.
- The insights from those already running multi-million dollar...even billion dollar Evolved Enterprises.
- **Even World-Class ideas packaged and handed to you on a Silver Platter so you can bring them to life.**

We have been working so hard on this, every member of my team has stepped up in a BIG way, because I really believe **the world needs you & your unique contribution to the global tapestry.**

And I am willing to put my own money, my resources, my team, and my list of contacts on table for the right Evolved Enterprises that come along. Get all the details here -

www.EvolvedEnterprise.com/10000ideas

Selected Recommended Reading
for Evolved Entrepreneurs

Reinventing Organizations
– Frederic Laloux

Peak – Chip Conley

Screw Business as Usual
– Sir Richard Branson

POW! Right Between the Eyes! Profiting from the Power of Surprise
– Andy Nulman

Make It Big! 49 Secrets for Building a Life of Extreme Success
– Frank McKinney

Daring Greatly – Brene Brown

Delivering Happiness
– Tony Hsieh

Start Something That Matters
– Blake Mycoskie

Looptail – Bruce Poon Tip

The Power of Full Engagement
– Jim Loehr and Tony Schwartz

The Business of Happiness
– Ted Leonsis

Unique Ability® 2.0: Discovery
– Catherine Nomura, Julia Waller, and Shannon Waller

Success Through Stillness
– Russell Simmons

A Lapsed Anarchist's Approach to Building a Great Business
– Ari Weinzweig

Conscious Capitalism
– John Mackey and Raj Sisodia

Joy, Inc. – Richard Sheridan

Brains on Fire
– Robbin Phillips, Greg Cordell, Geno Church, and Spike Jones

The Great Work of Your Life
– Stephen Cope

Let's continue to explore the Evolved Enterprise™ and co-create these ideas to make them stronger, share more examples, and connect in a meaningful way. Join a free community Facebook group and uncover new resources here:

www.EvolvedEnterprise.org/resources